Need to Reach out?
colormecowgirl3@gmail.com

Be Bold, Get Creative and Help Bring These Cowgirls Back to Life in "COLOR ME COWGIRL"

A special thank you to each and every one of the gals and photographers who contributed in the making of this coloring book.

This book was made to raise awareness of the human trafficking crisis in our country! The National Human Trafficking Hotline is available 24/7 and is confidential and multilingual:
1-888-373-7888
or text "help" to BEFREE (233733)

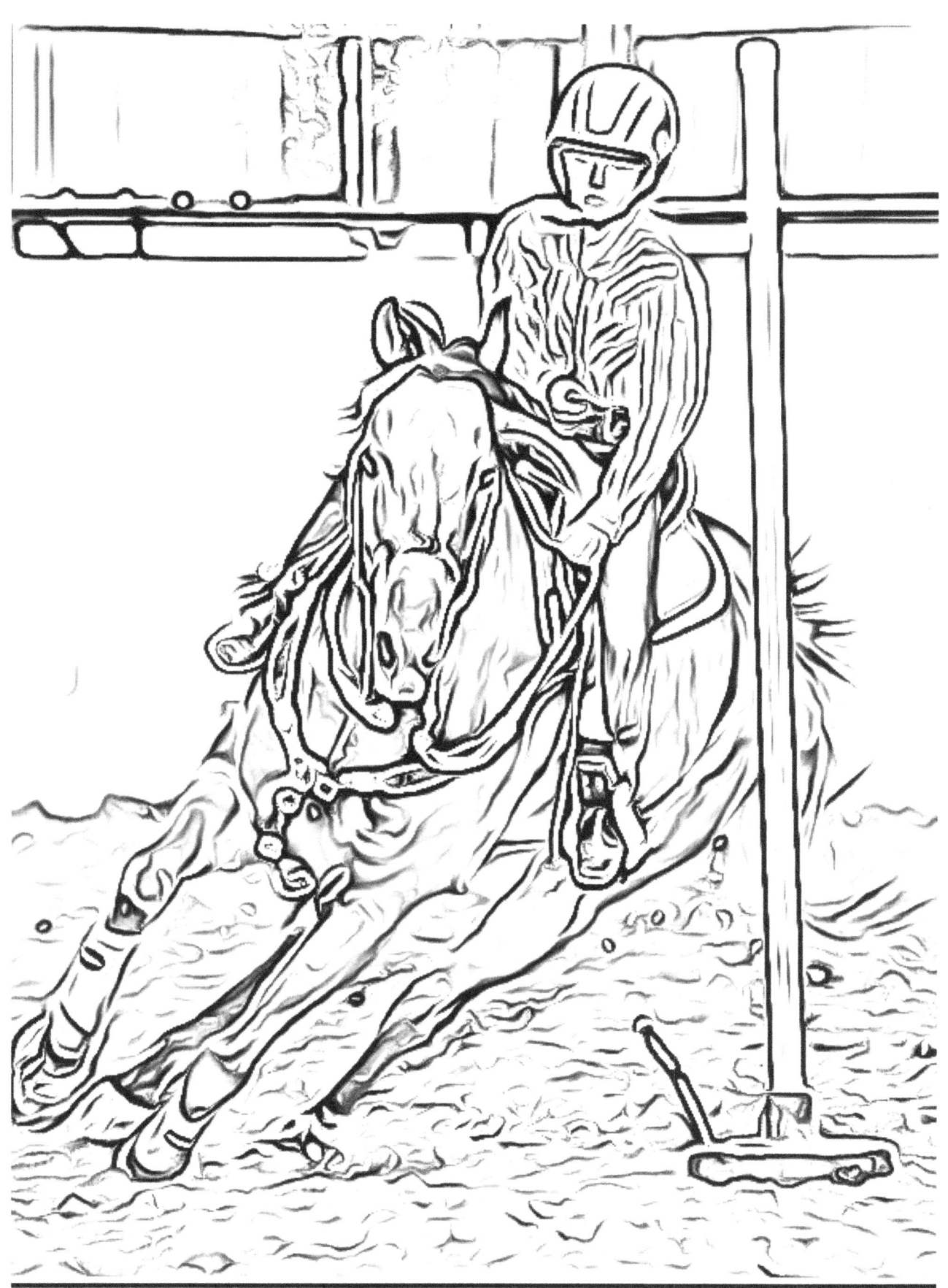

28

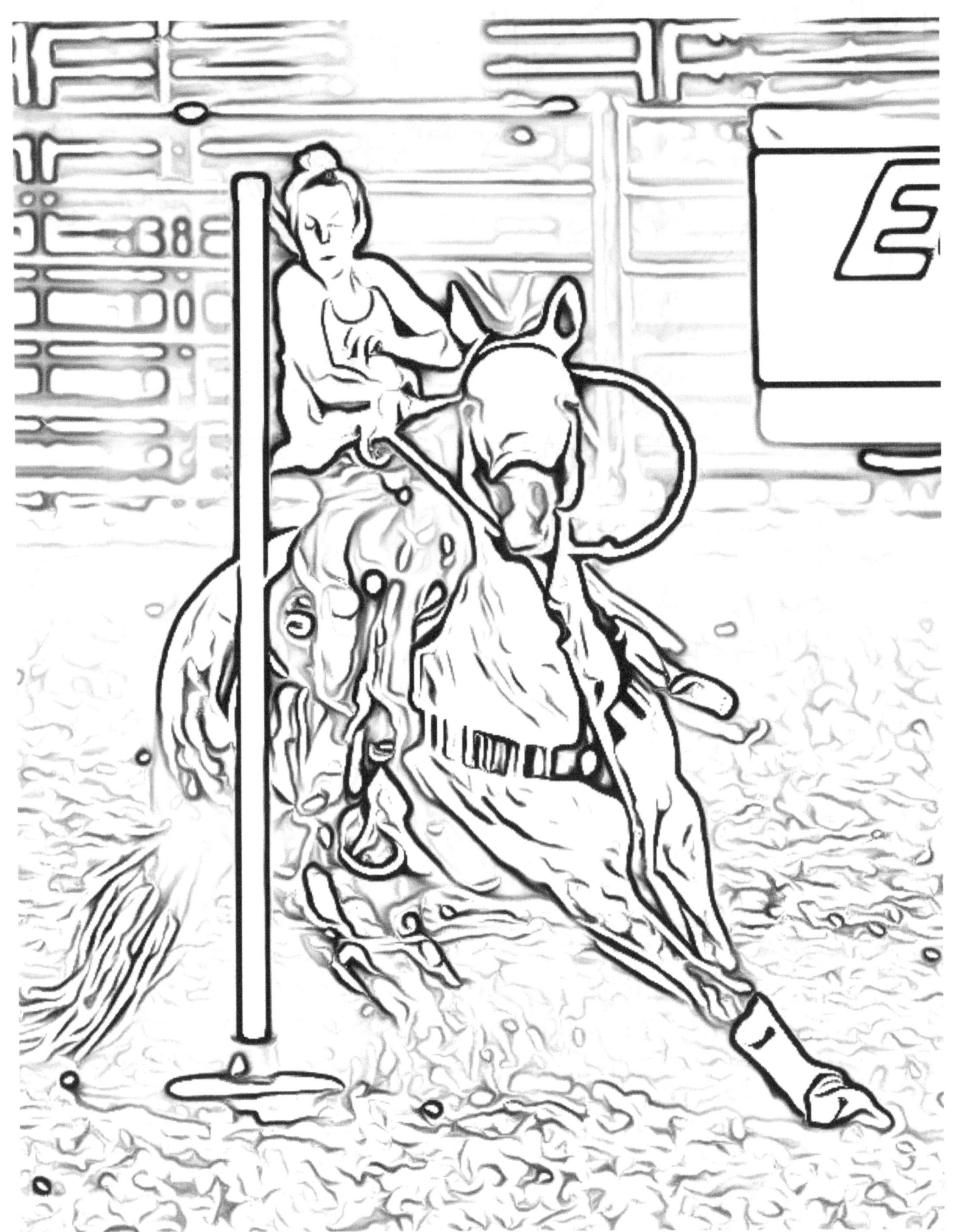

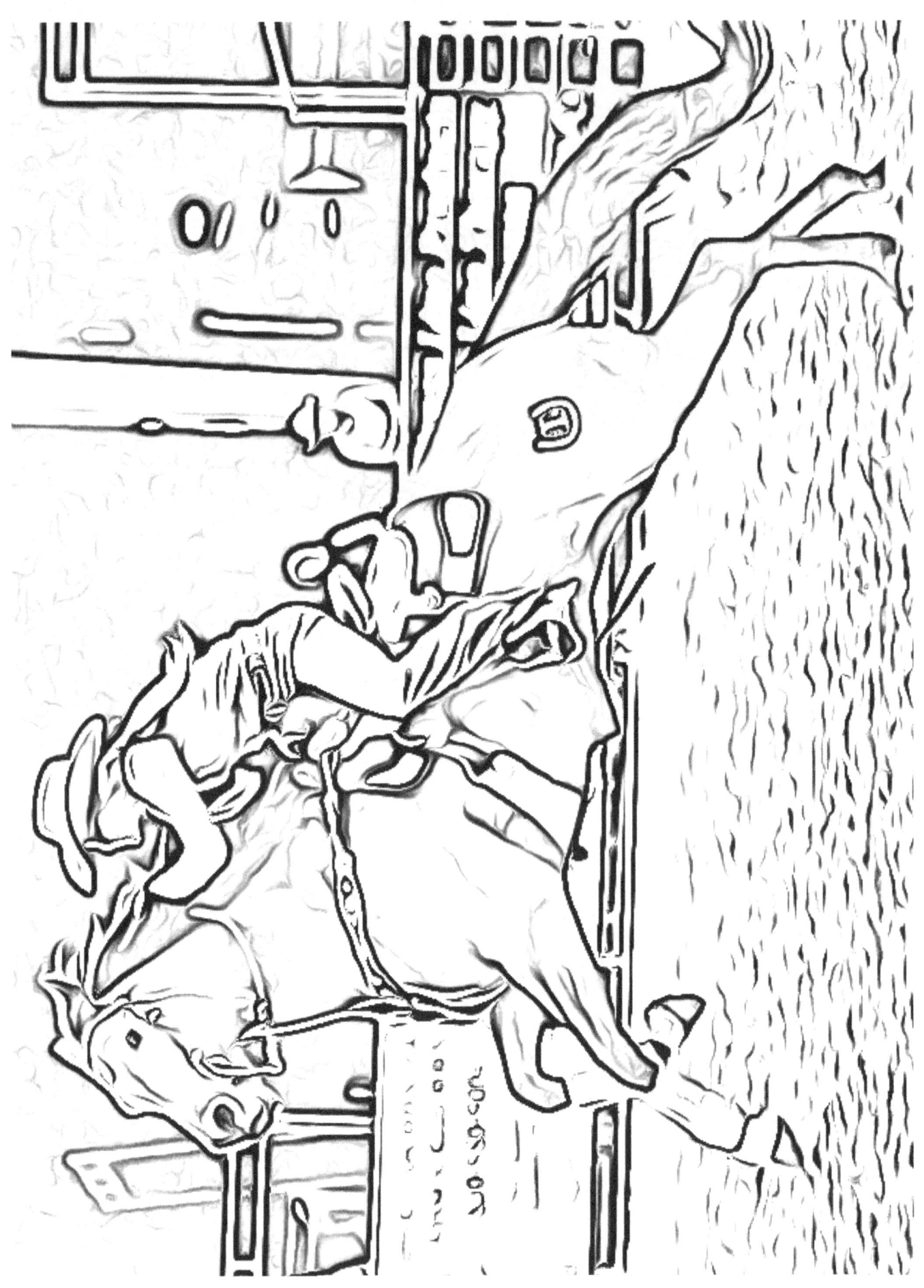

37

38

39

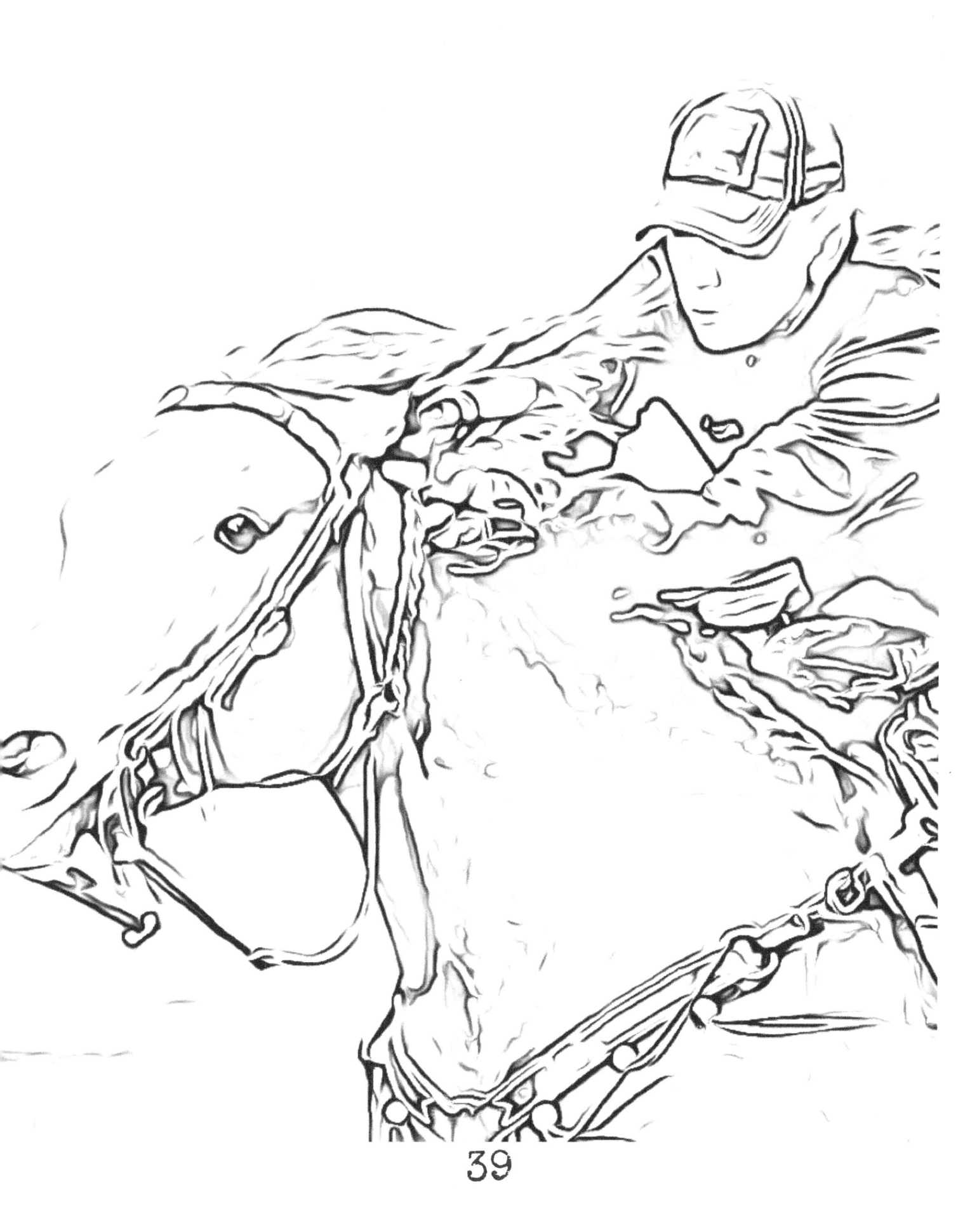

40

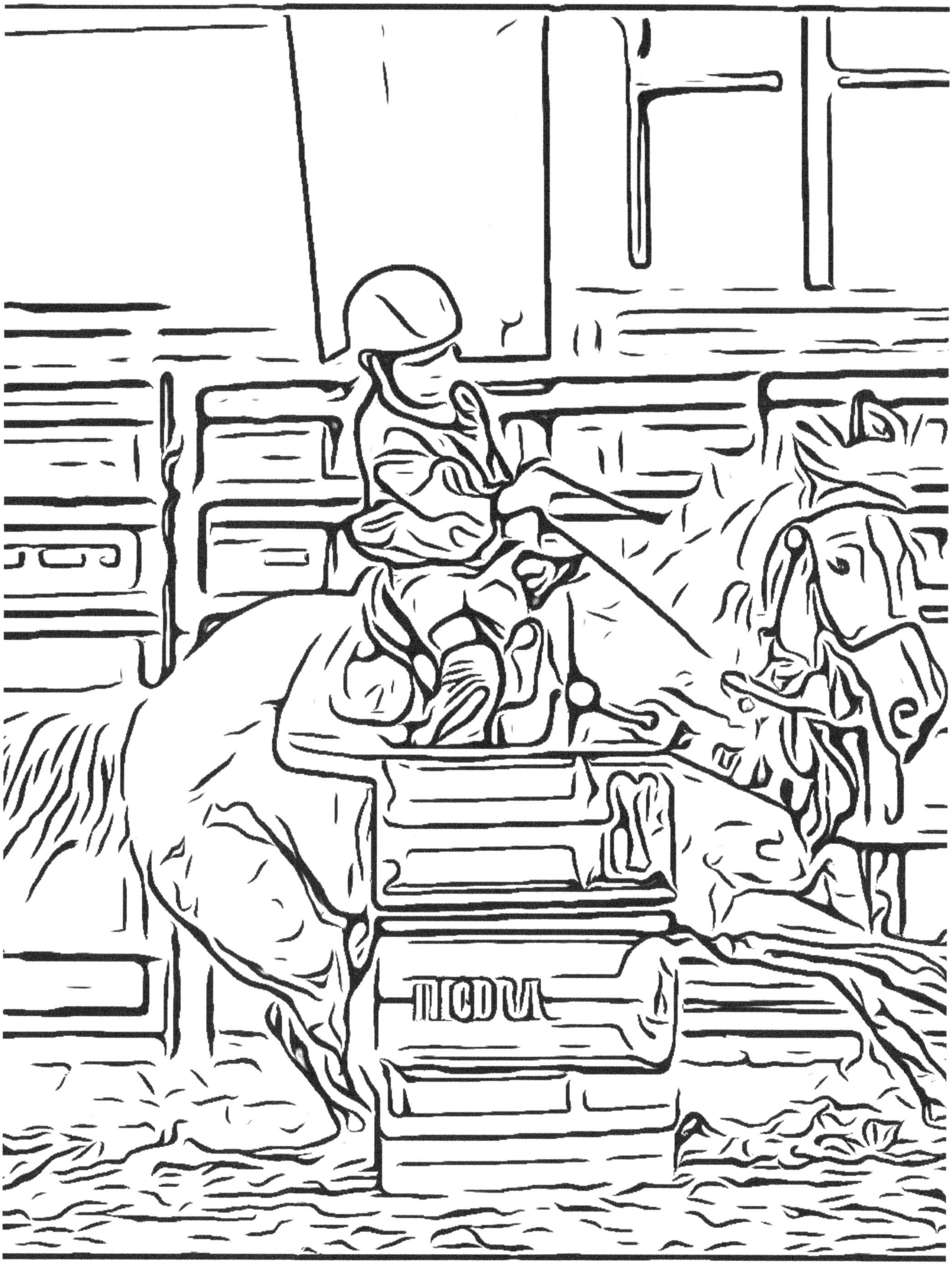

42

43

44

45

46

47

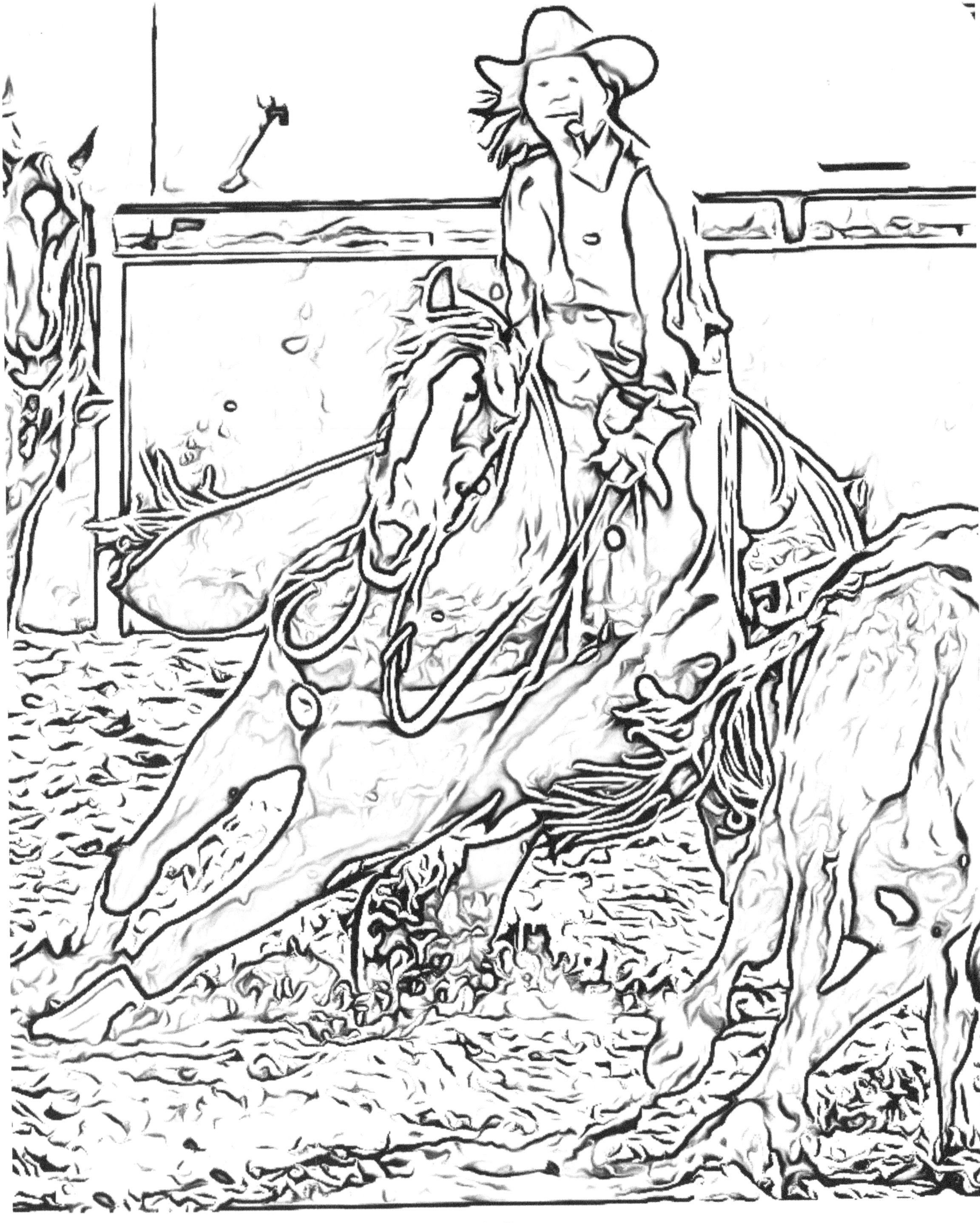

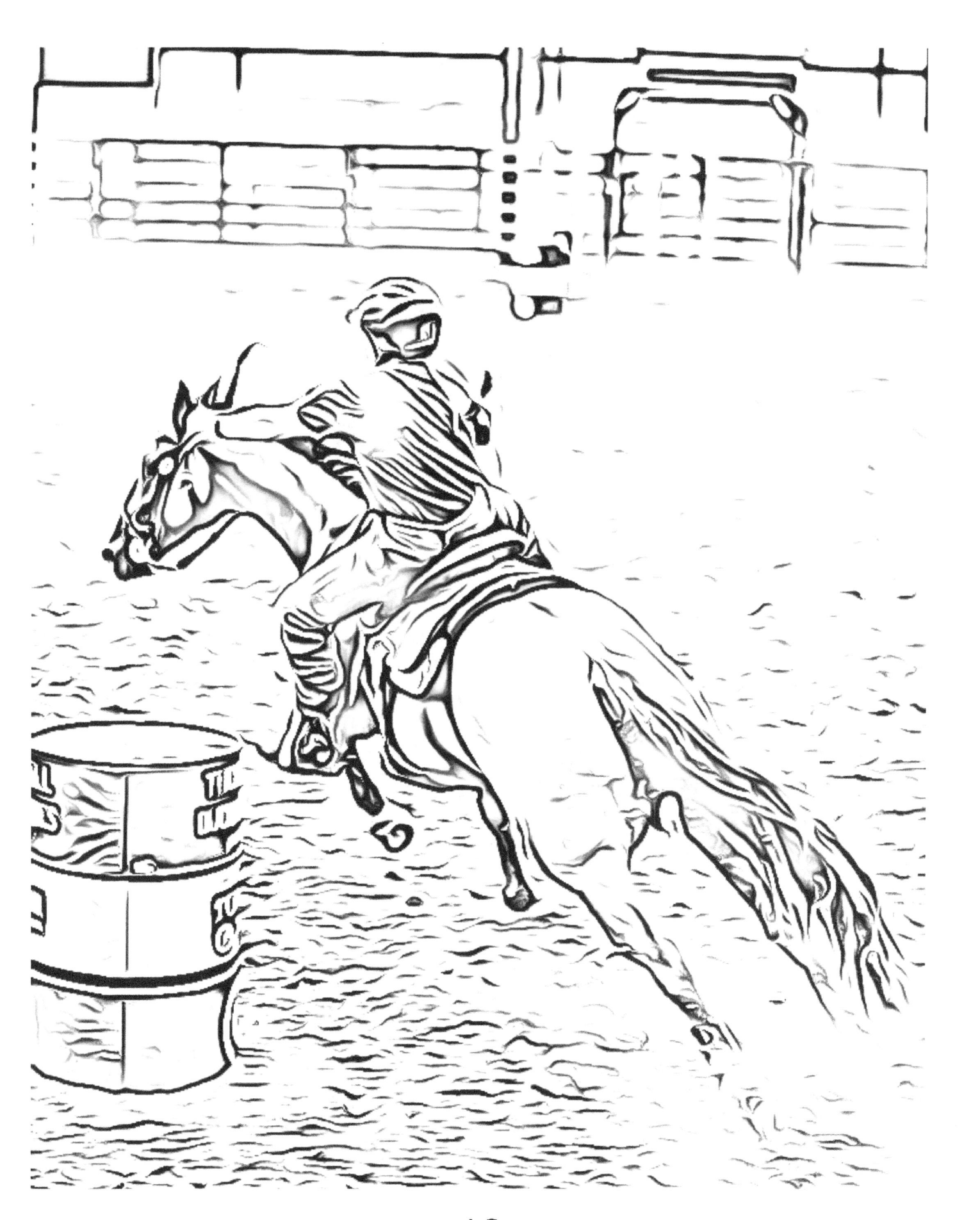

50

51

52

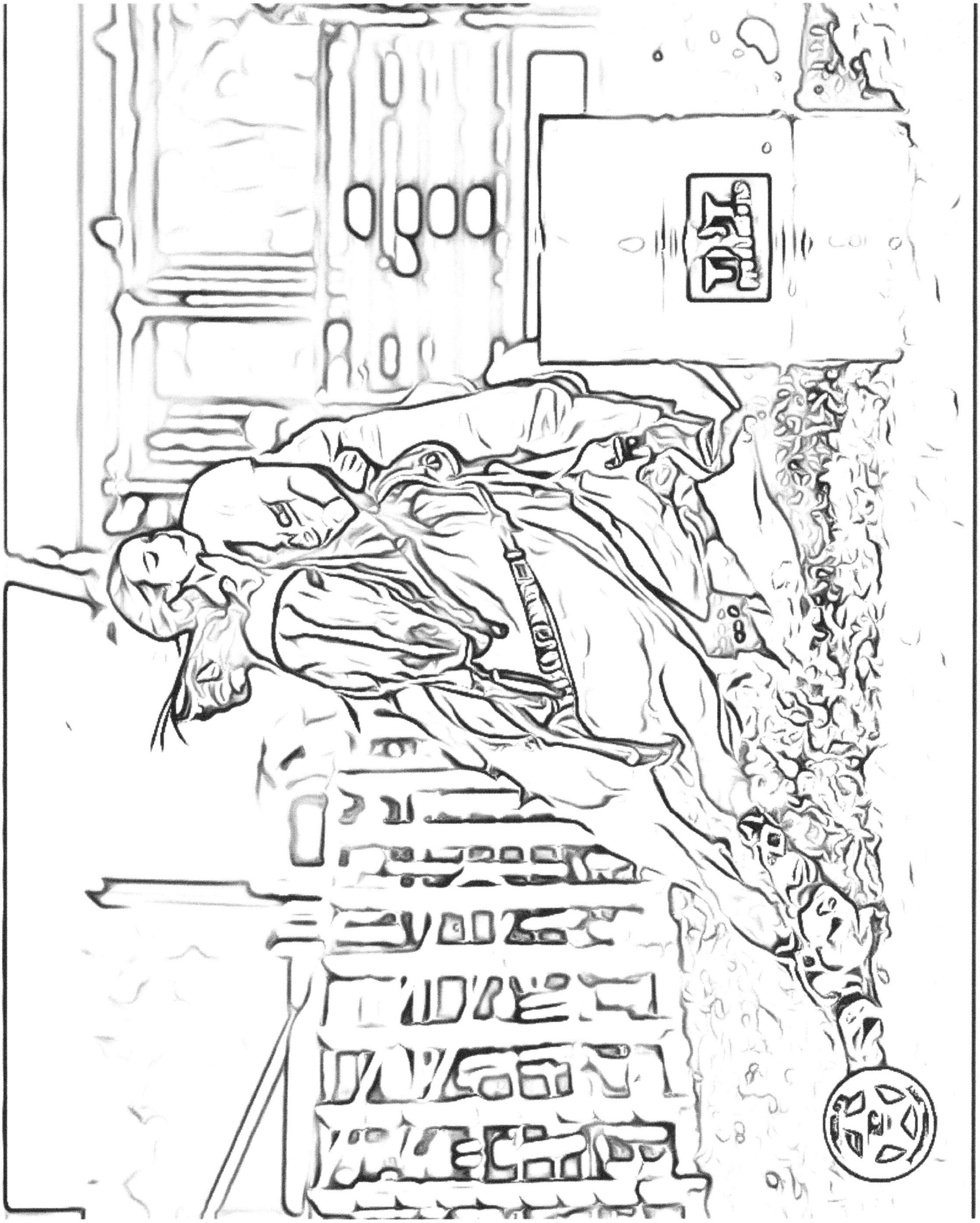

54

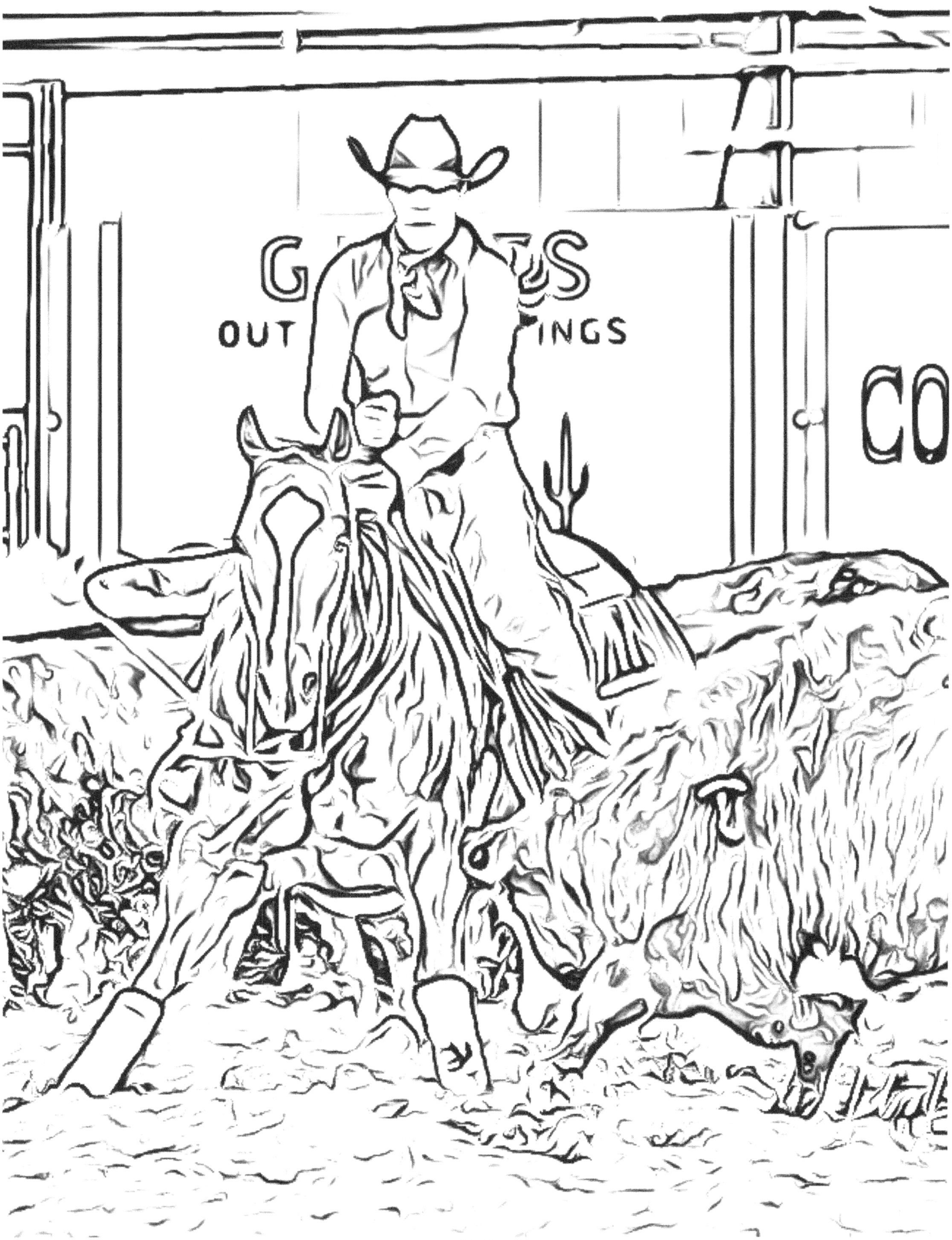
OUT
INGS
CO

56

57

58

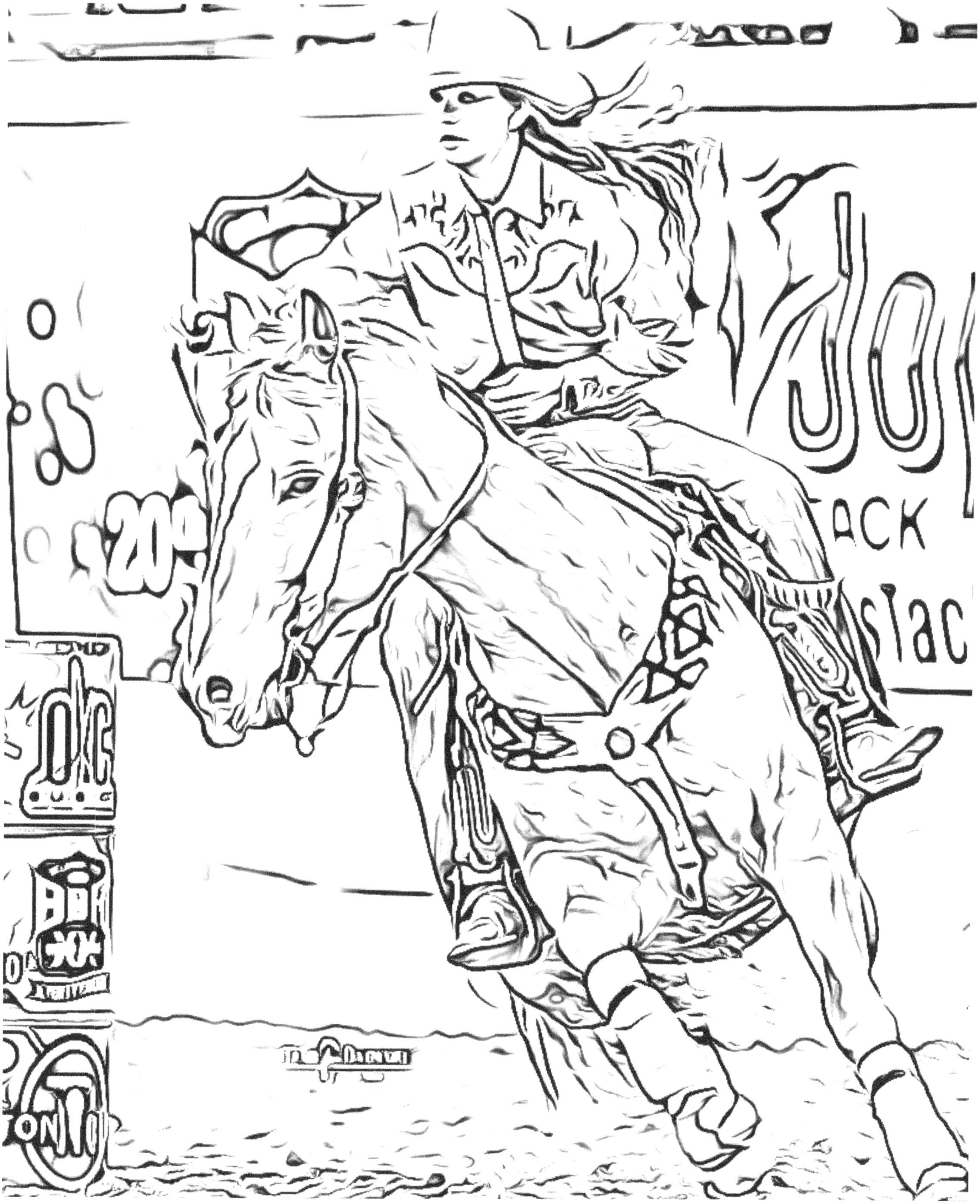

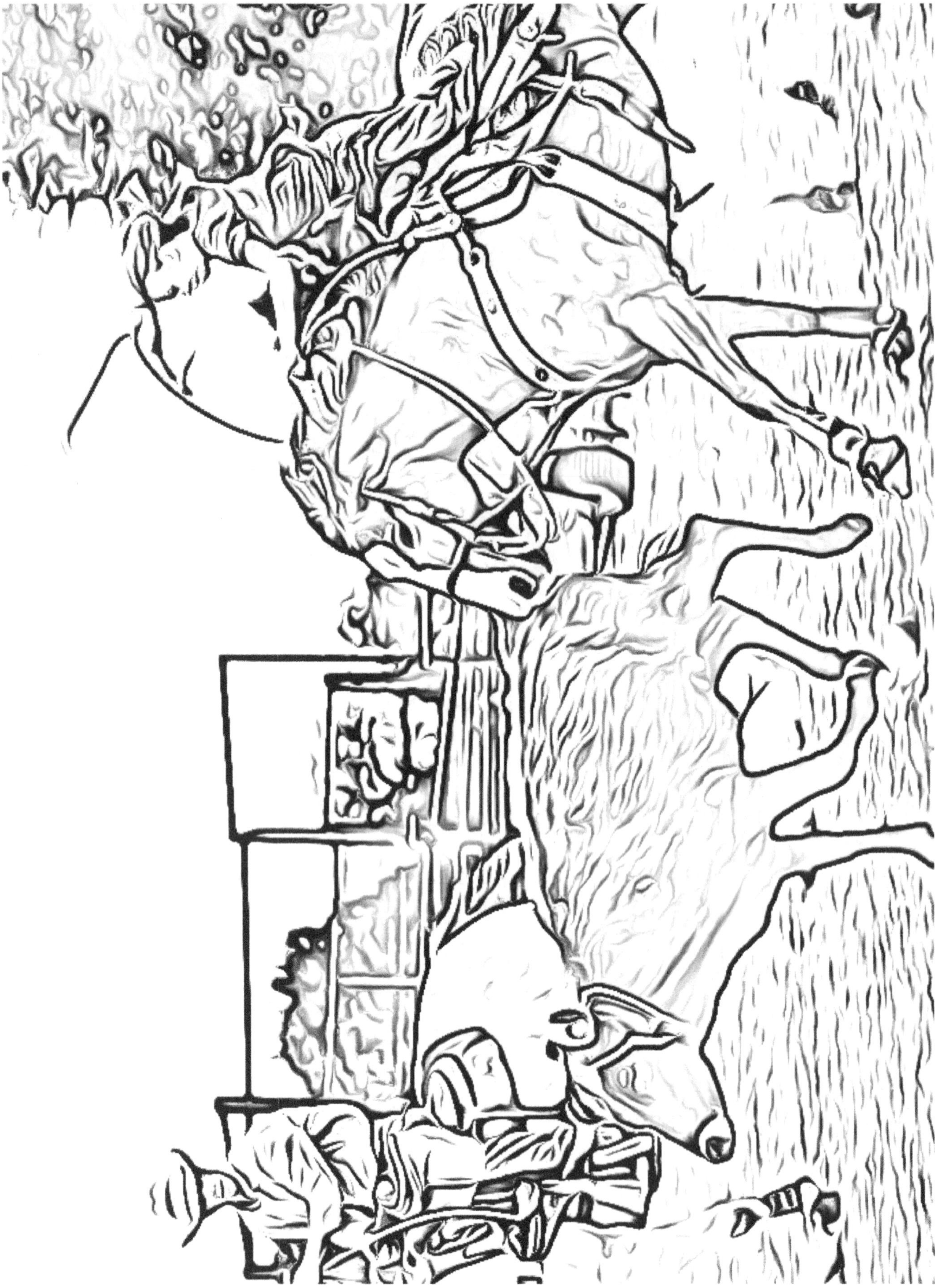

61

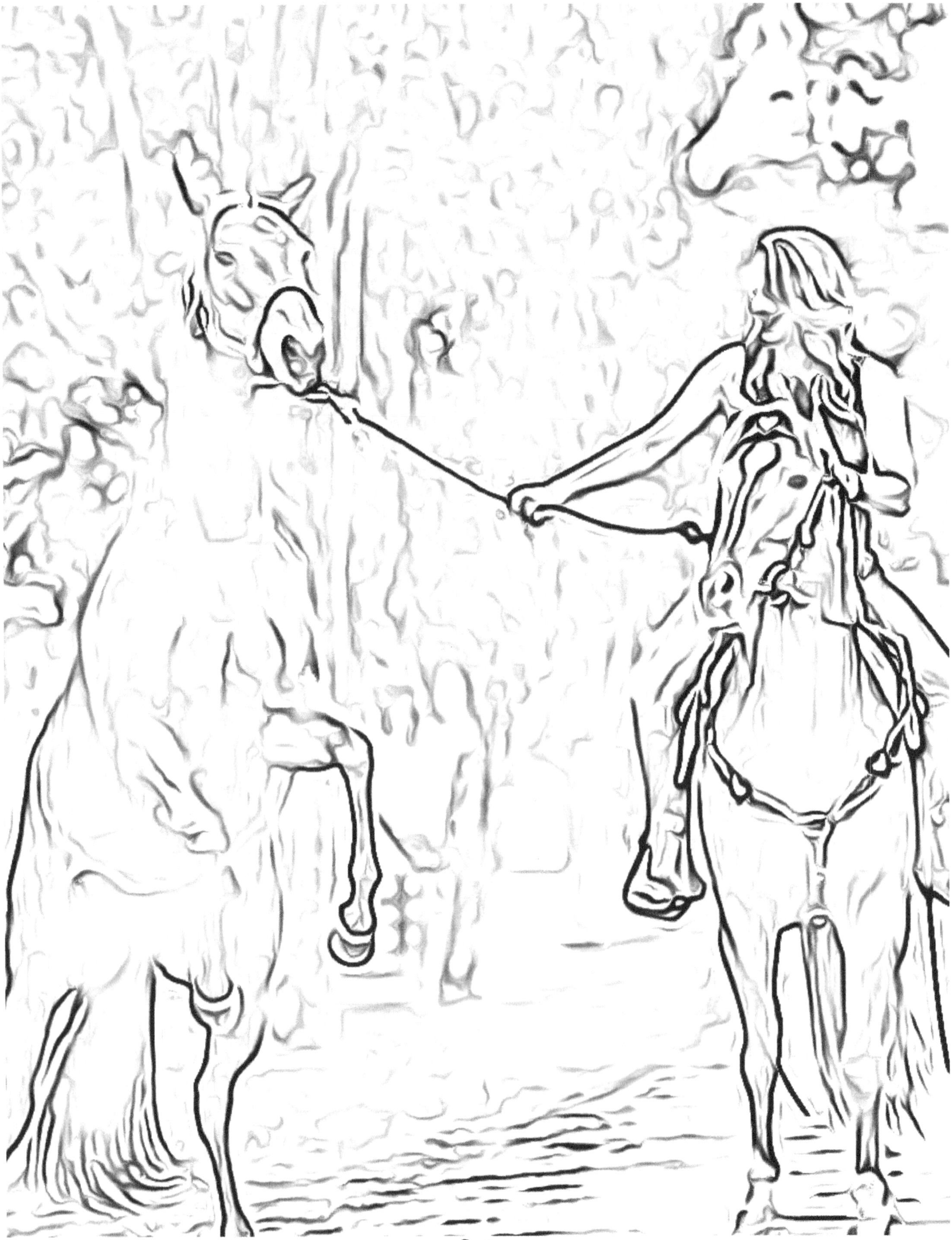

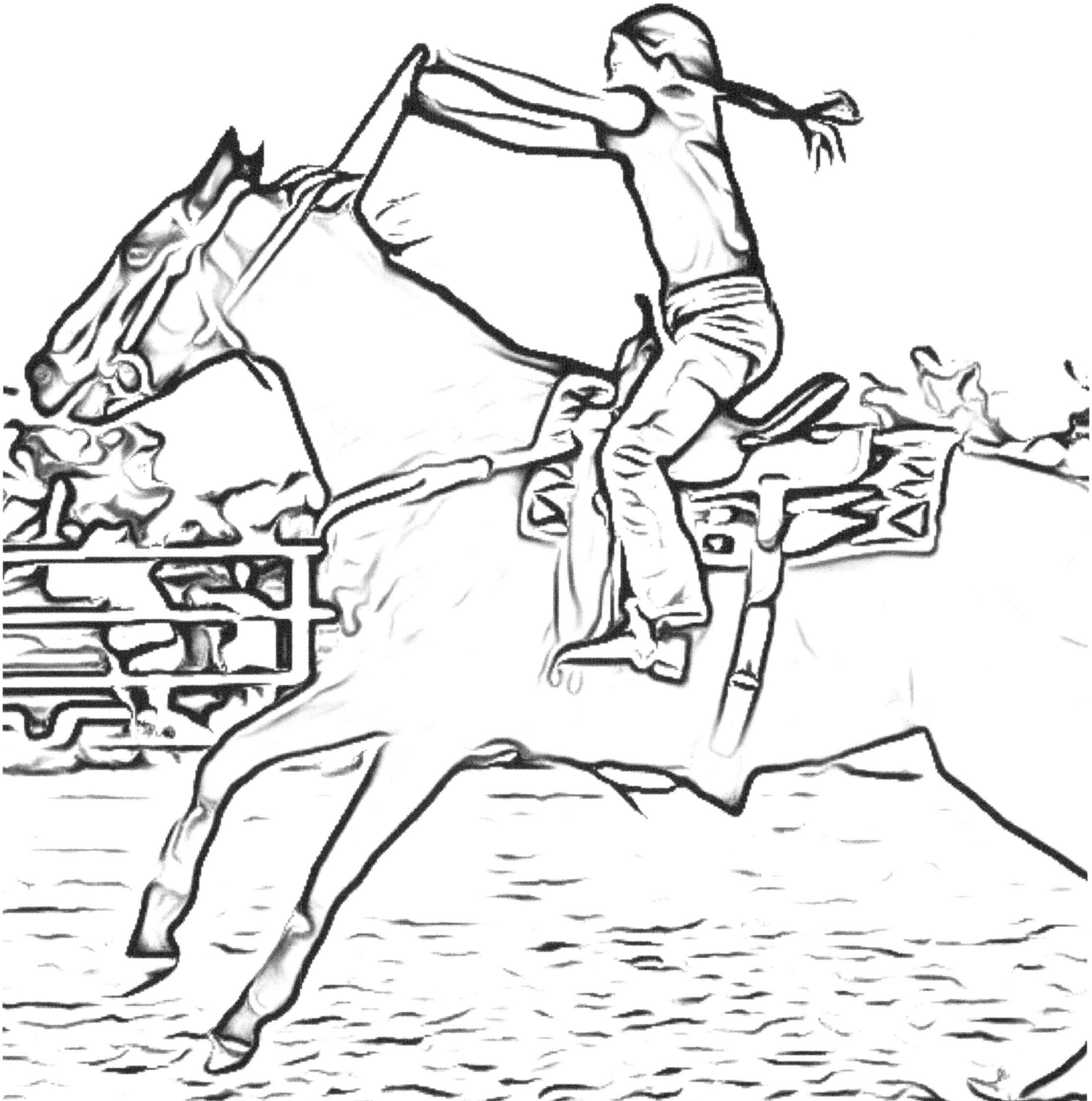

64

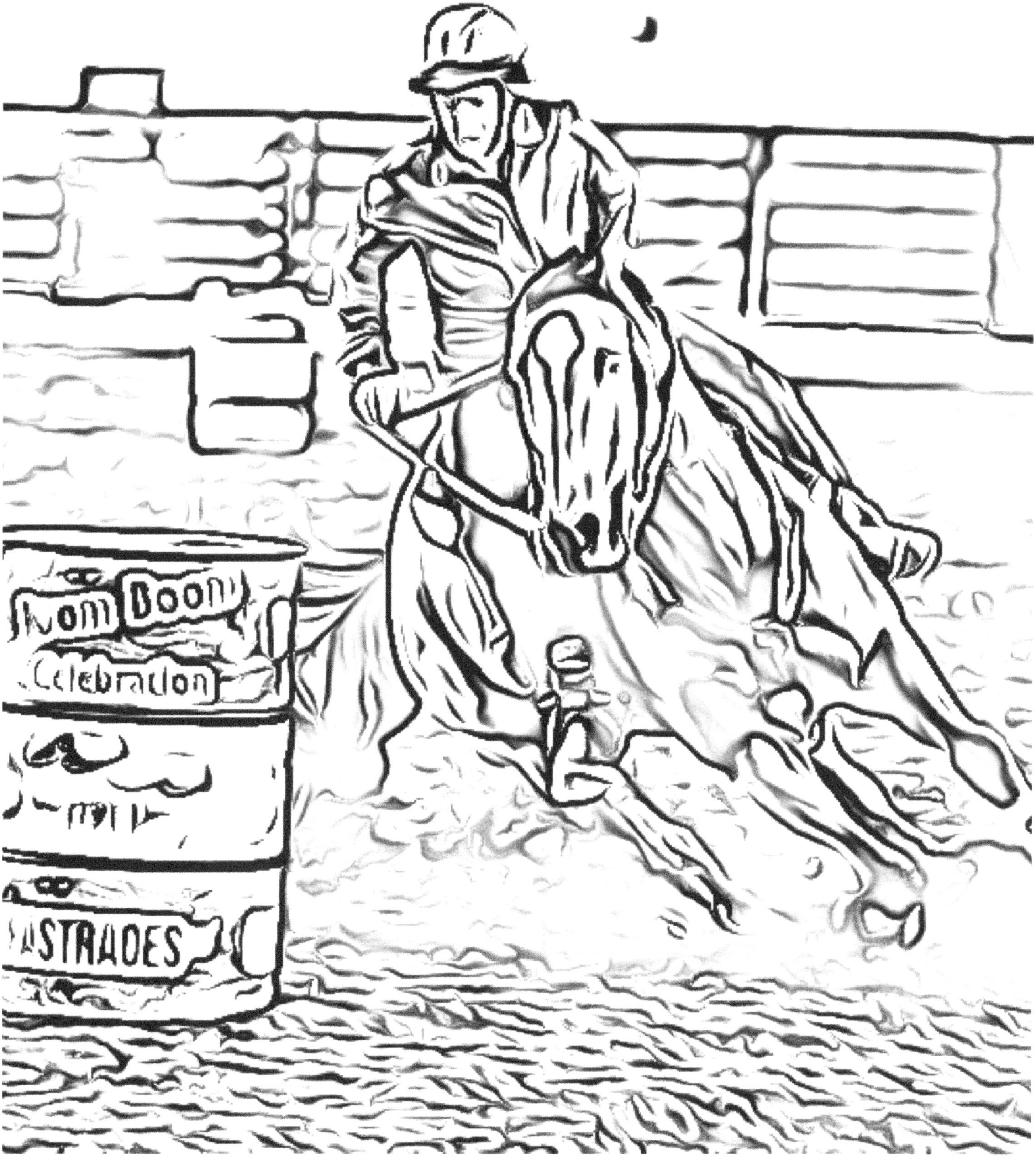
Celebration
STRADES

66

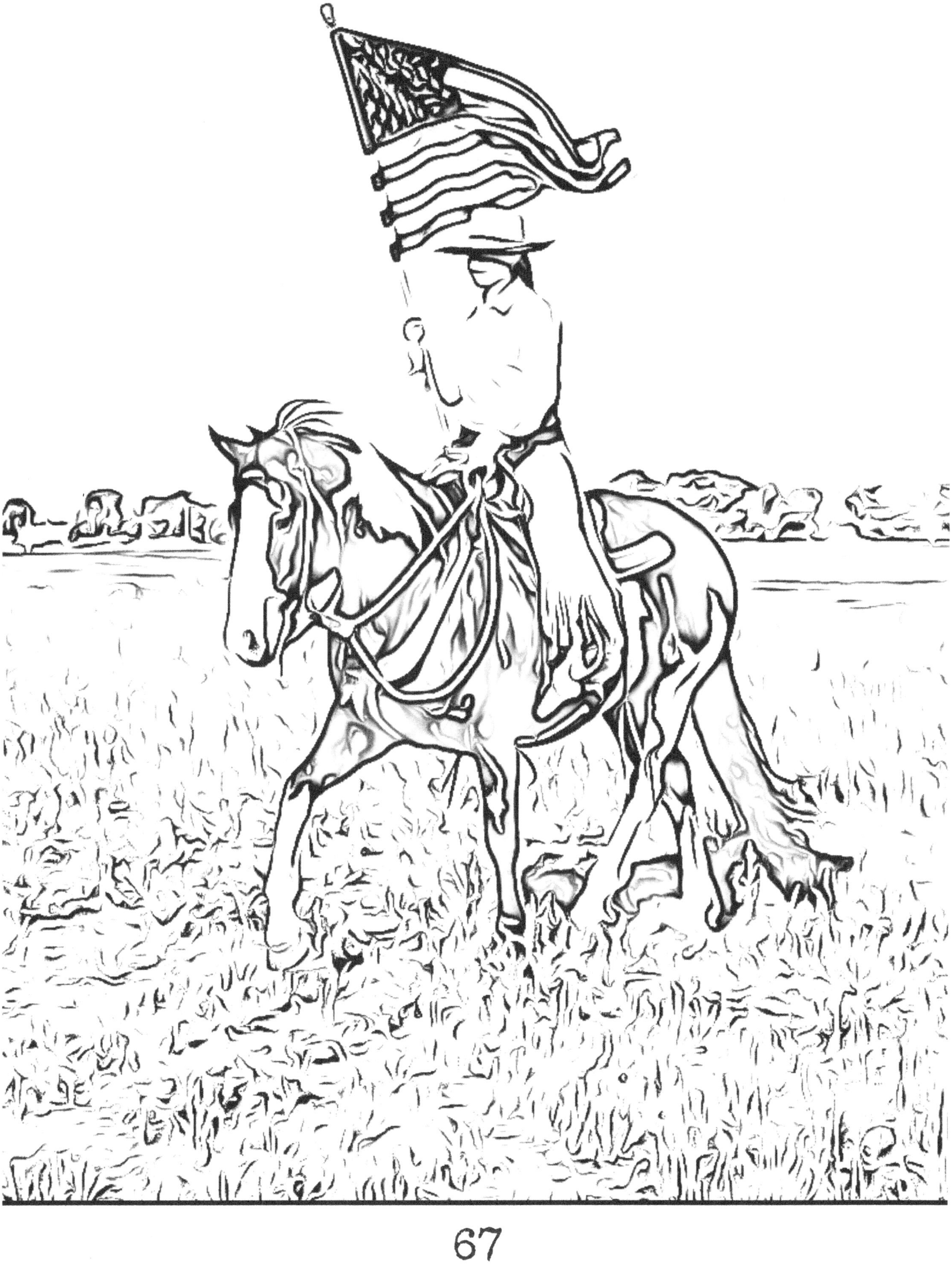

68

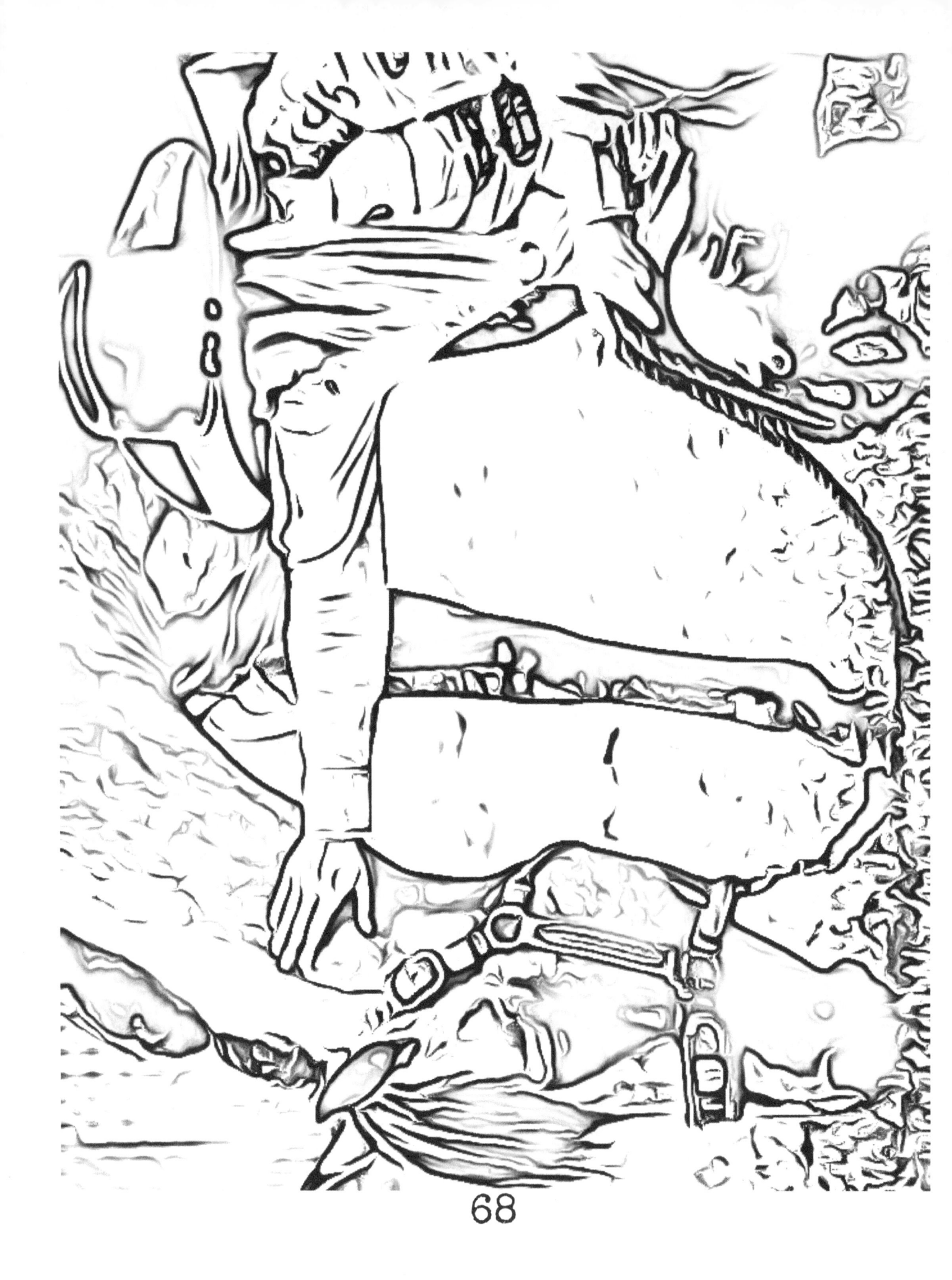

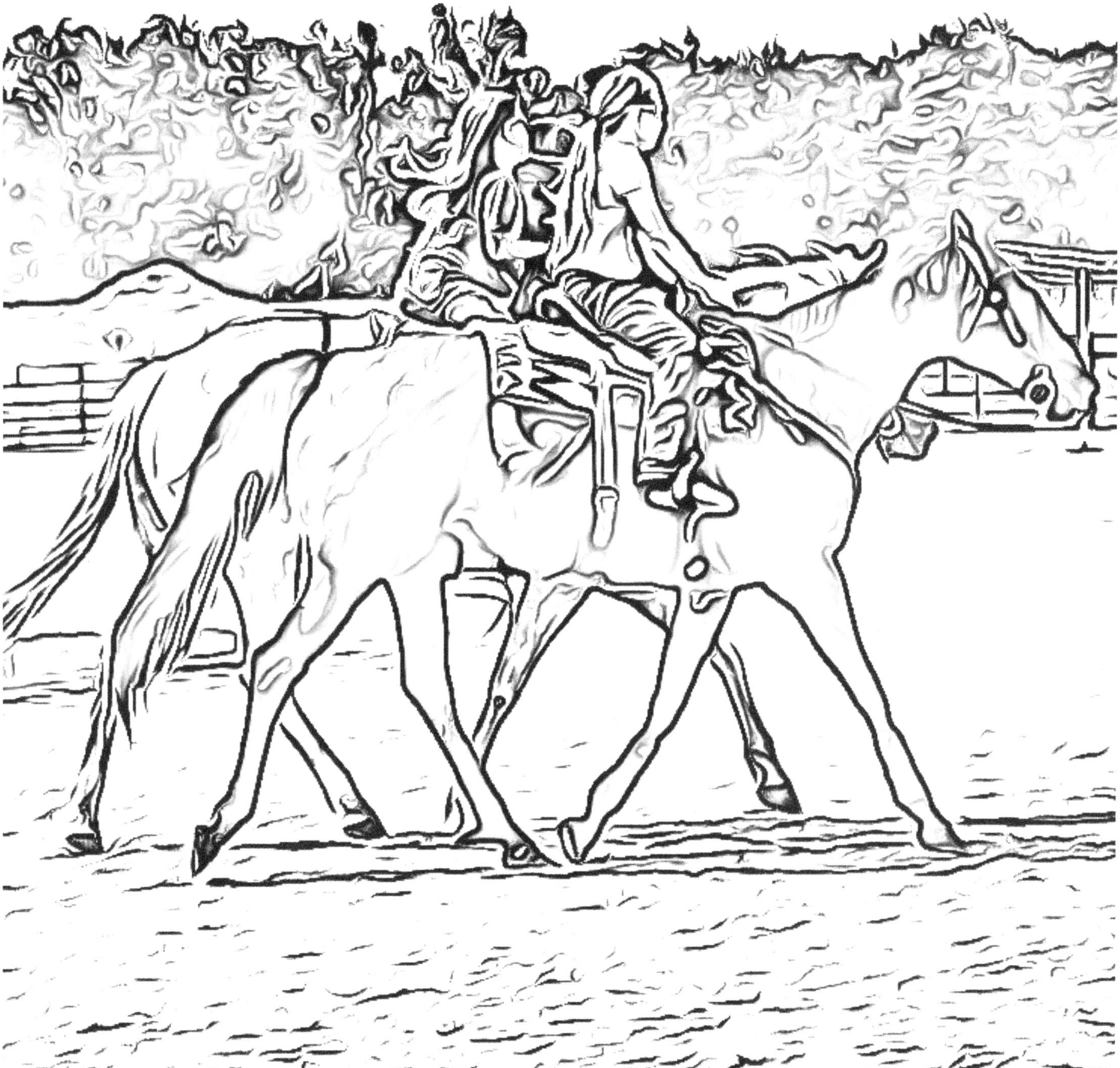

70

71

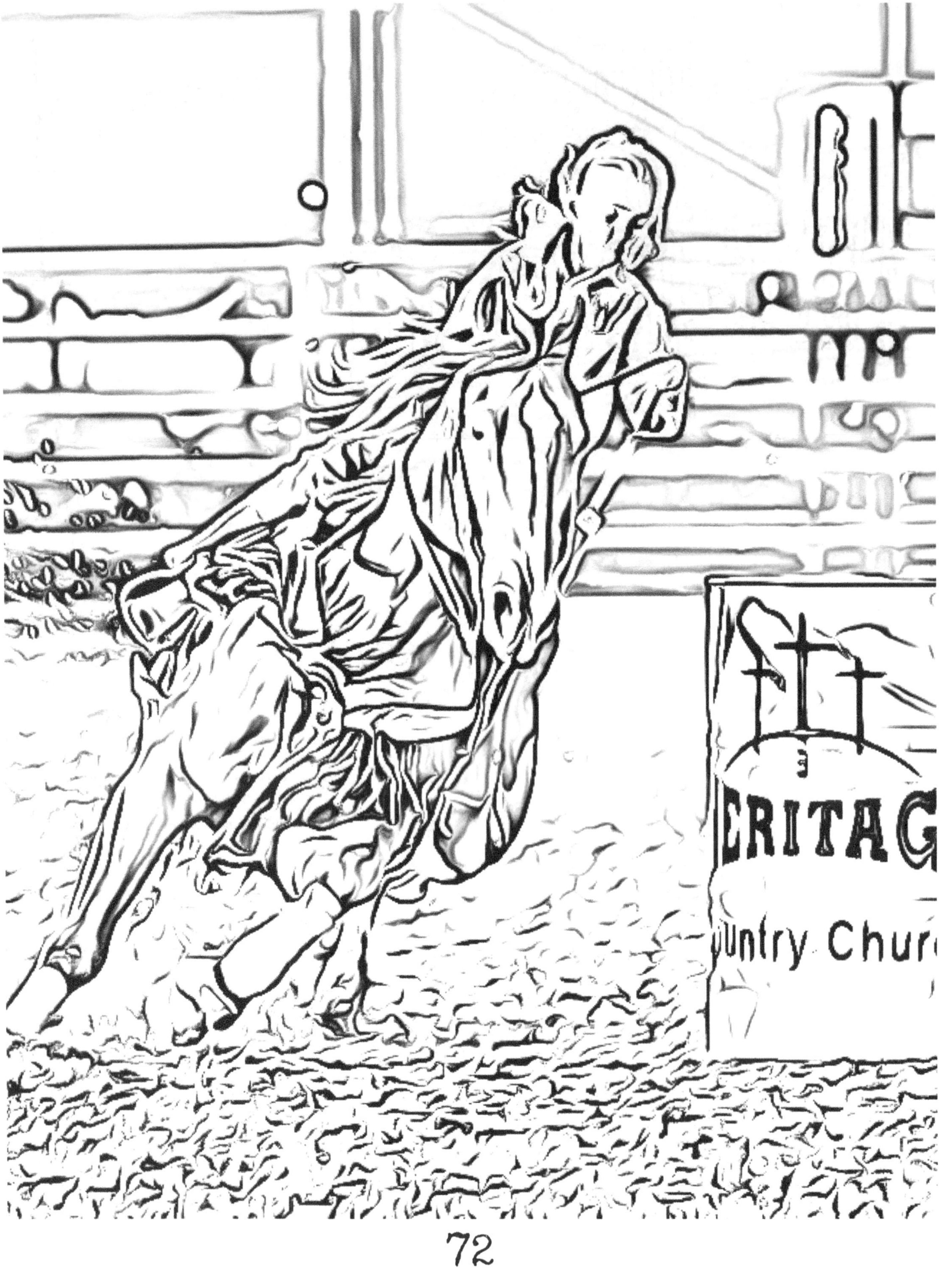
ERITAG
untry Churc

73

74

75

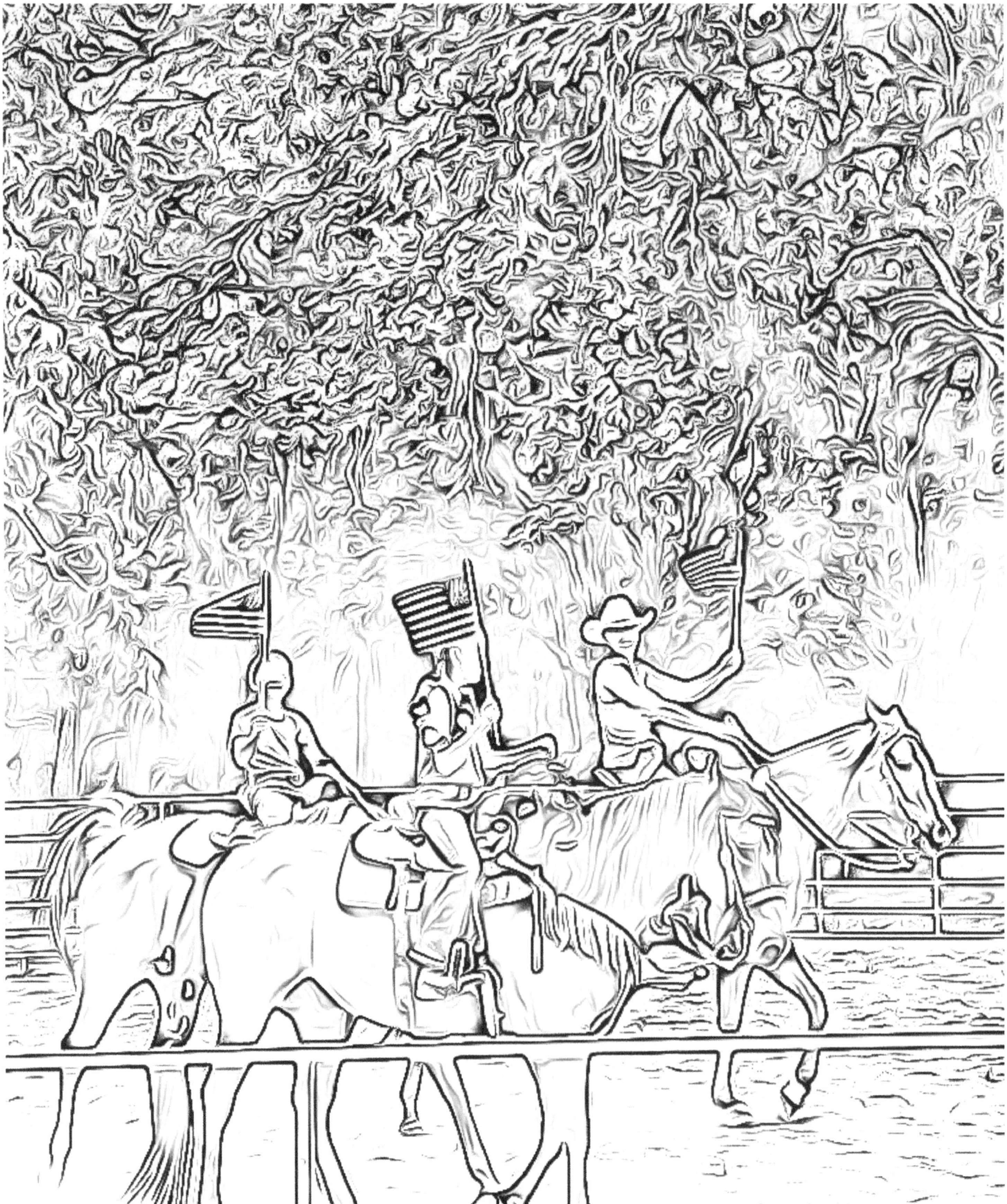

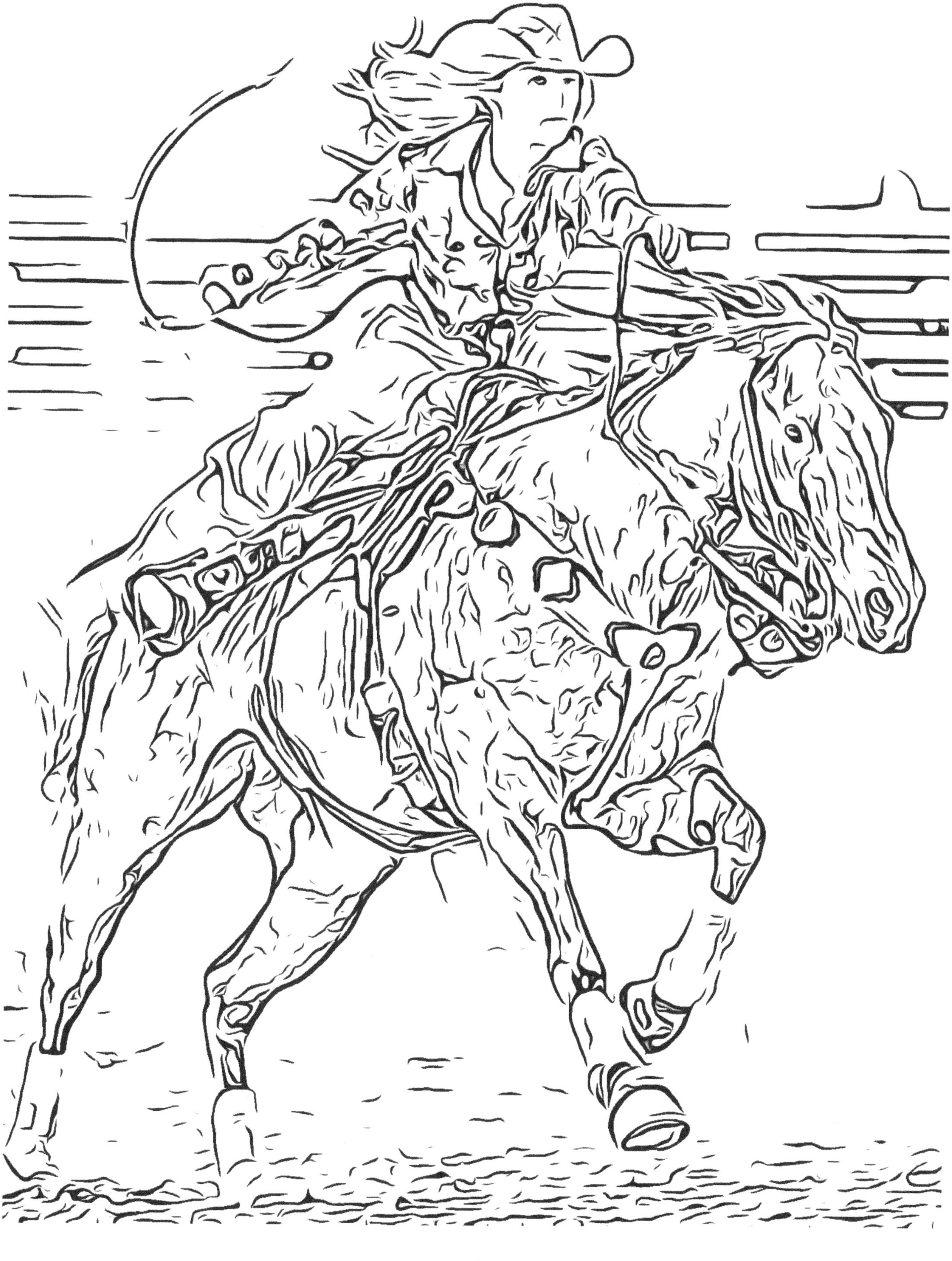

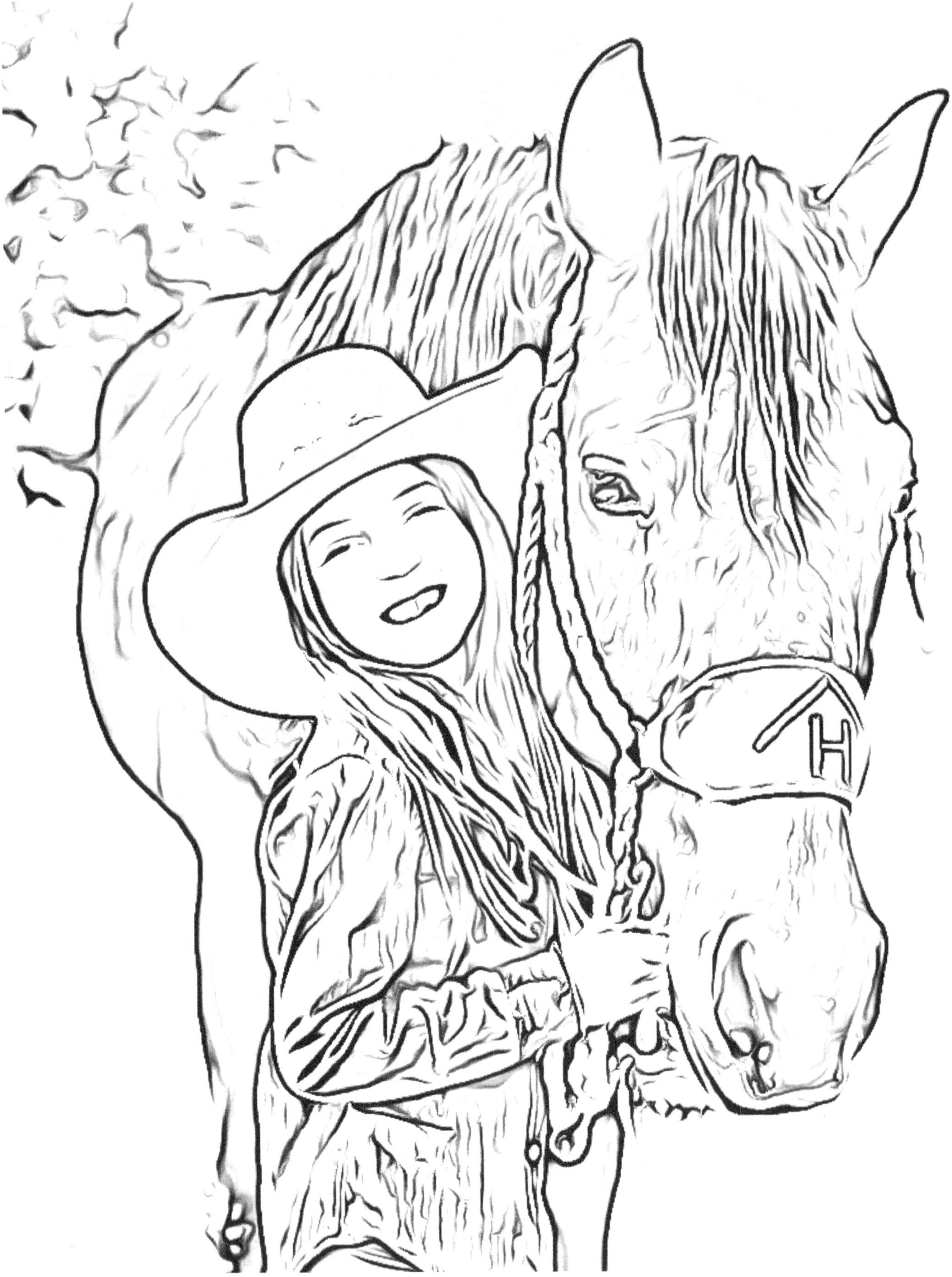
H

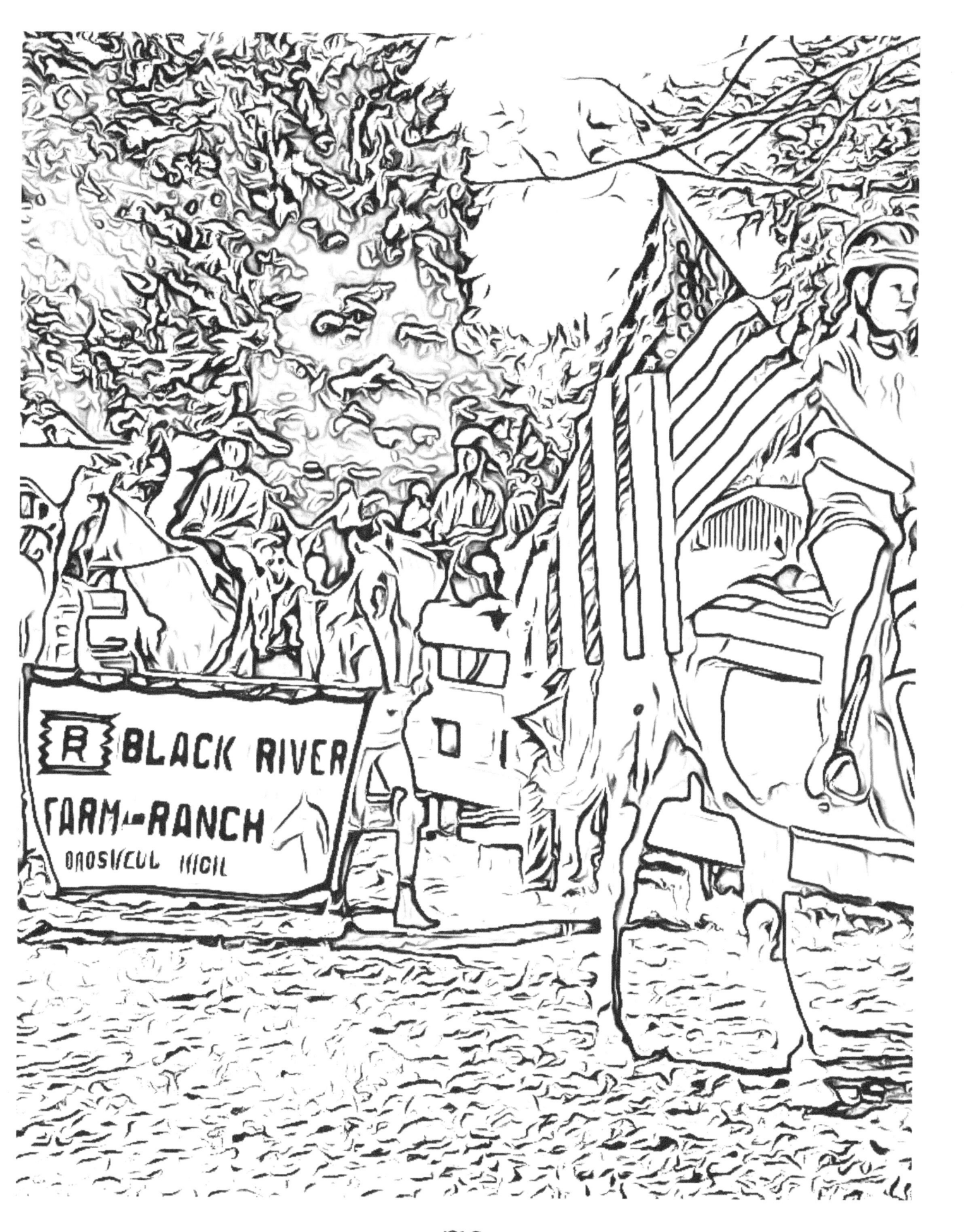
BLACK RIVER
FARM RANCH

80

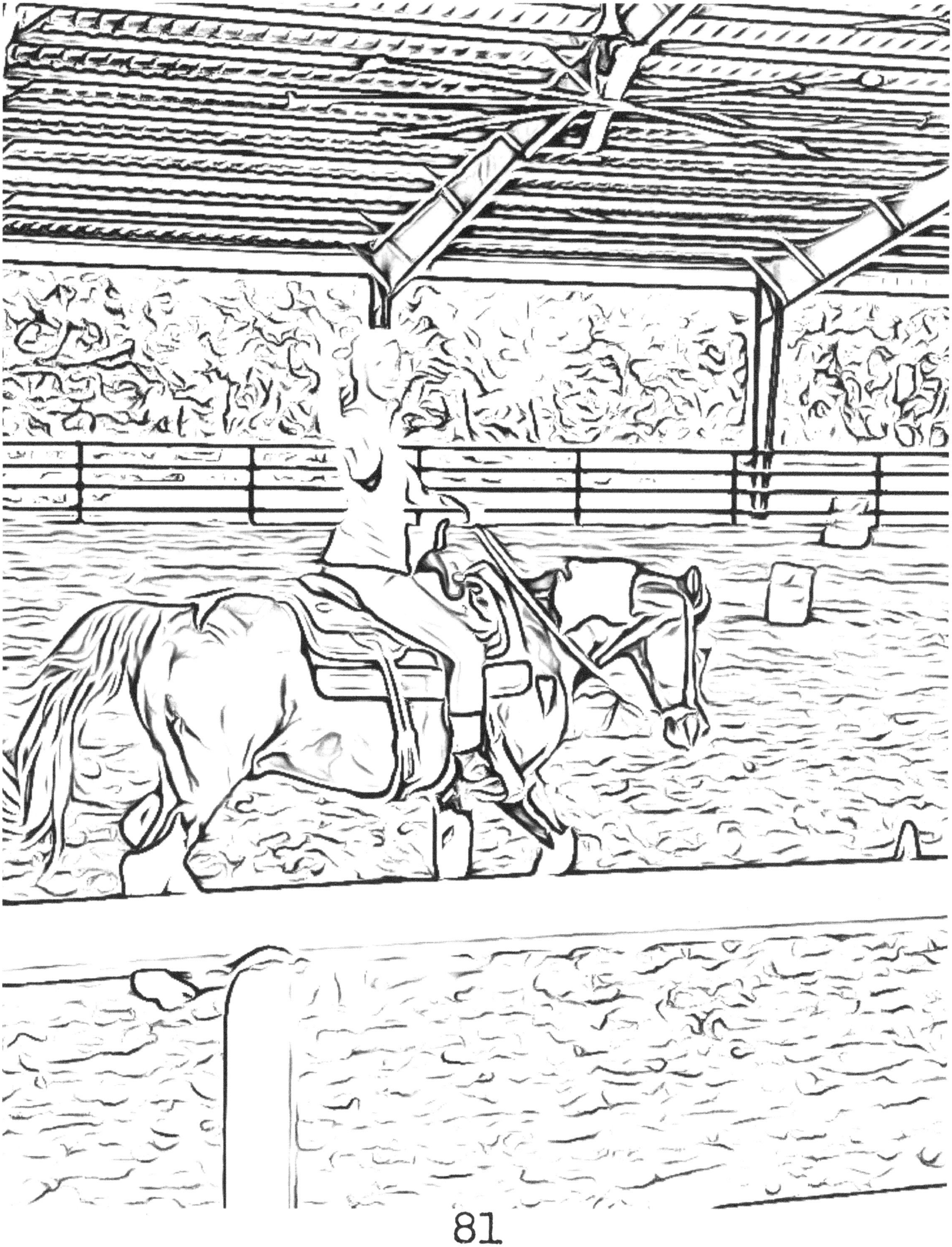

82

83

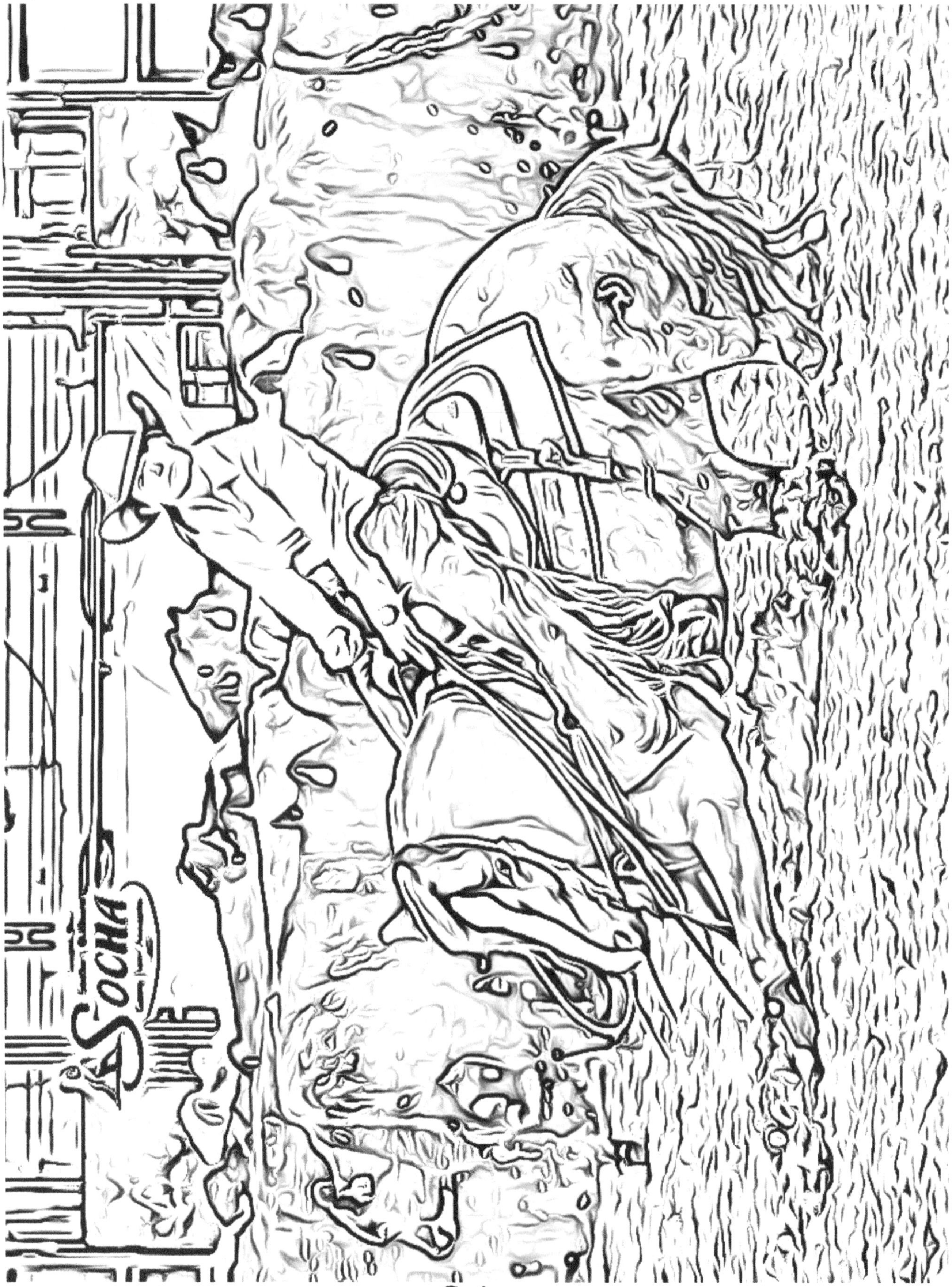
SOCHA

85

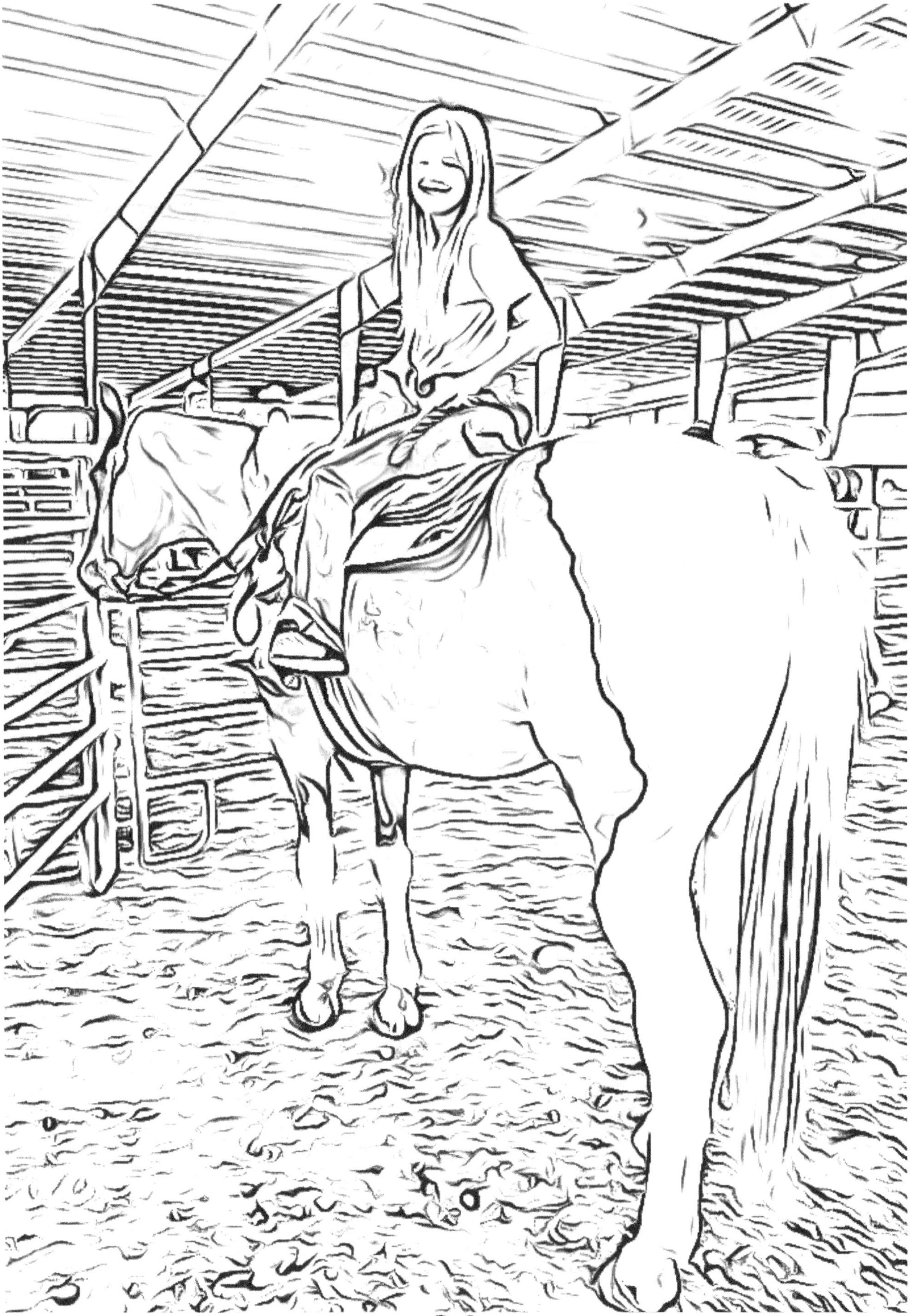

87

88

89

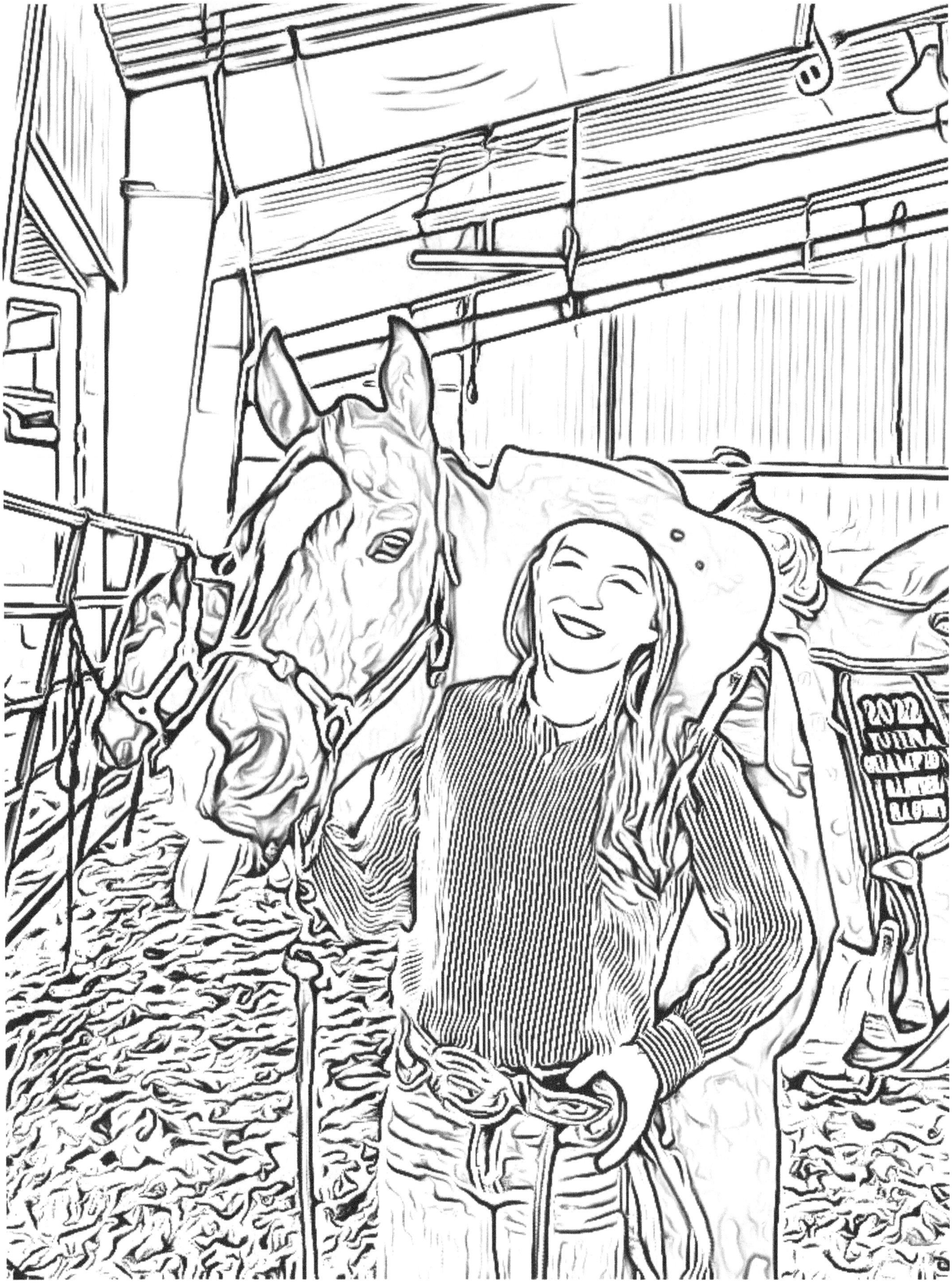
2022

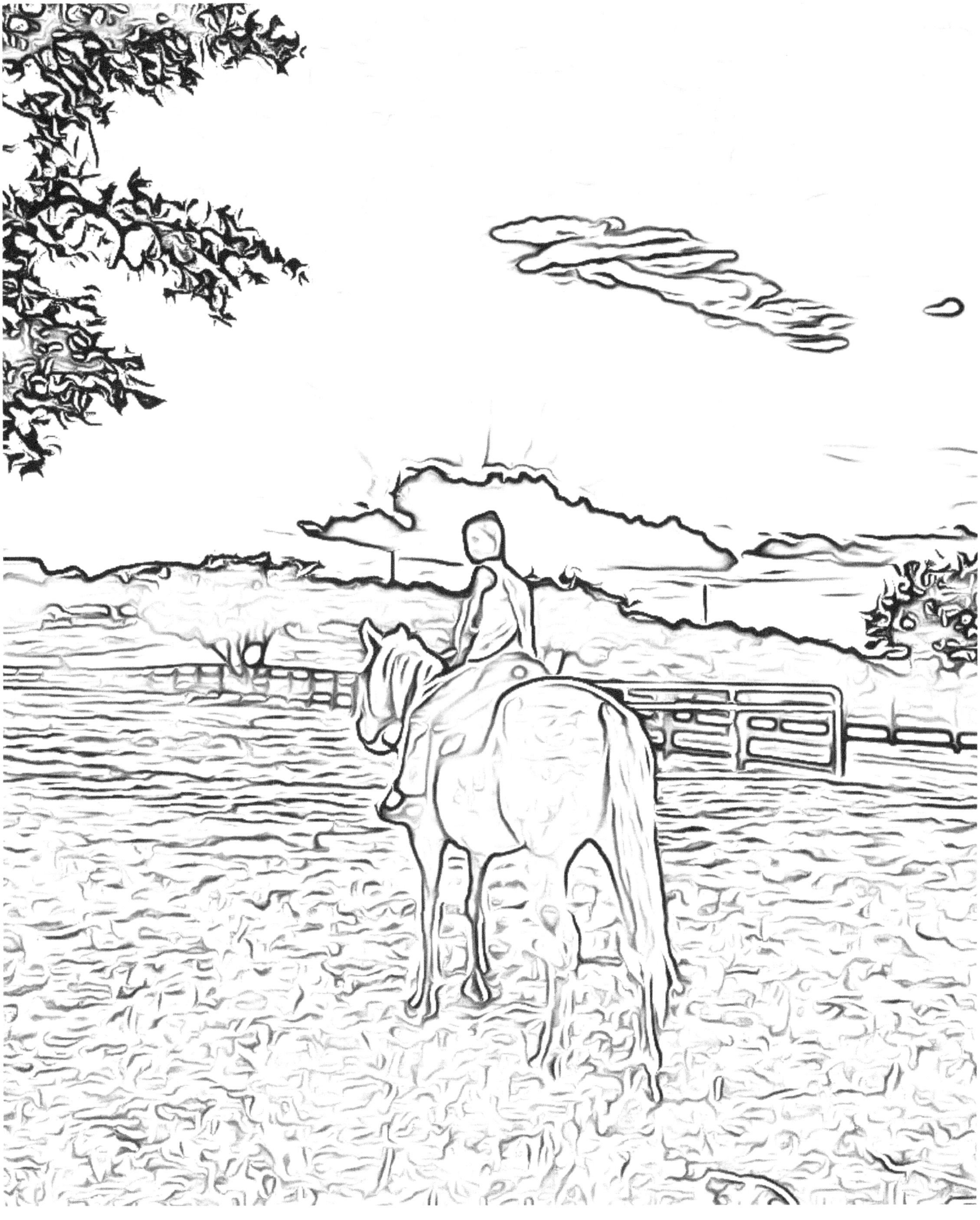

92

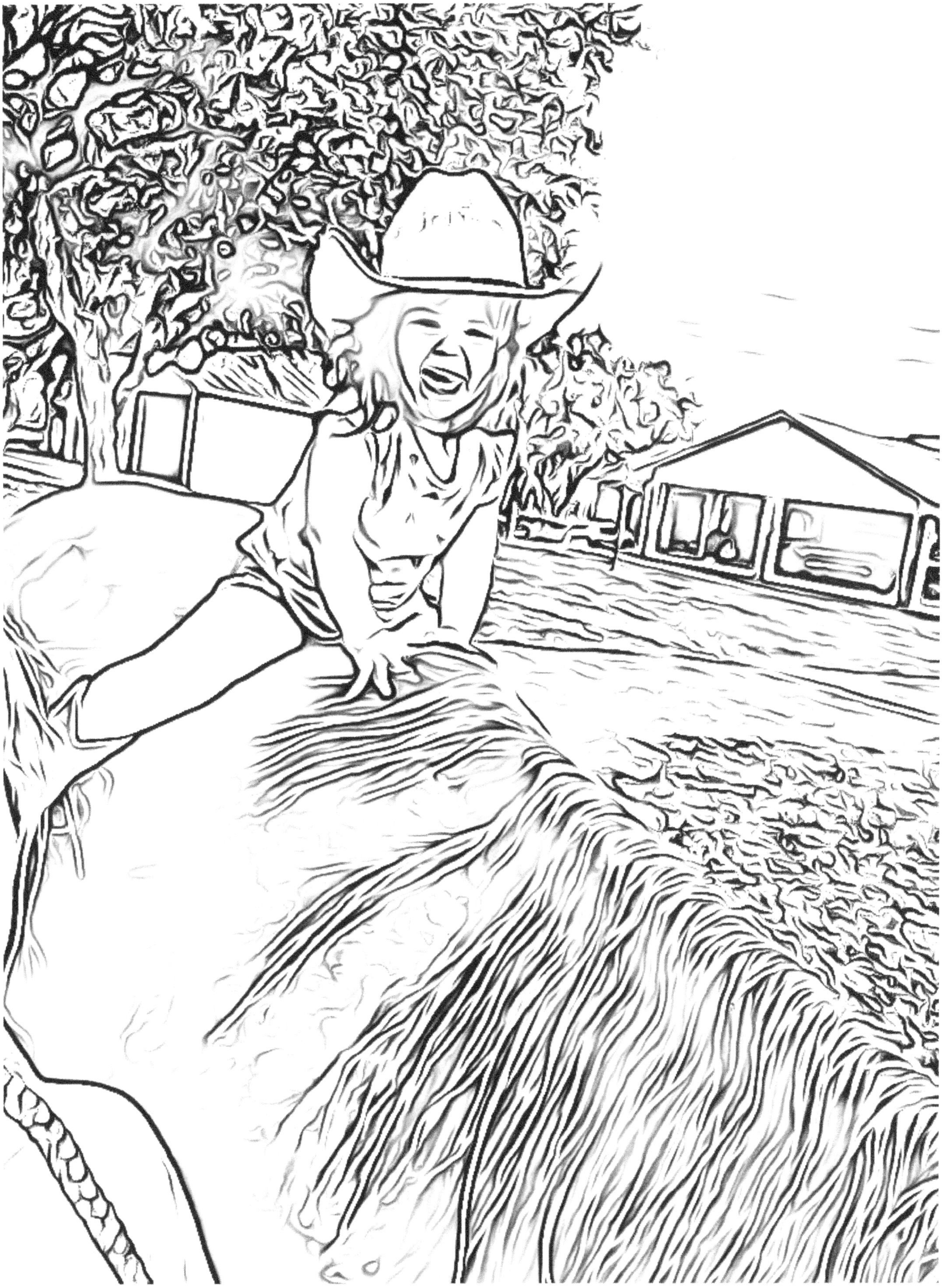

94

95

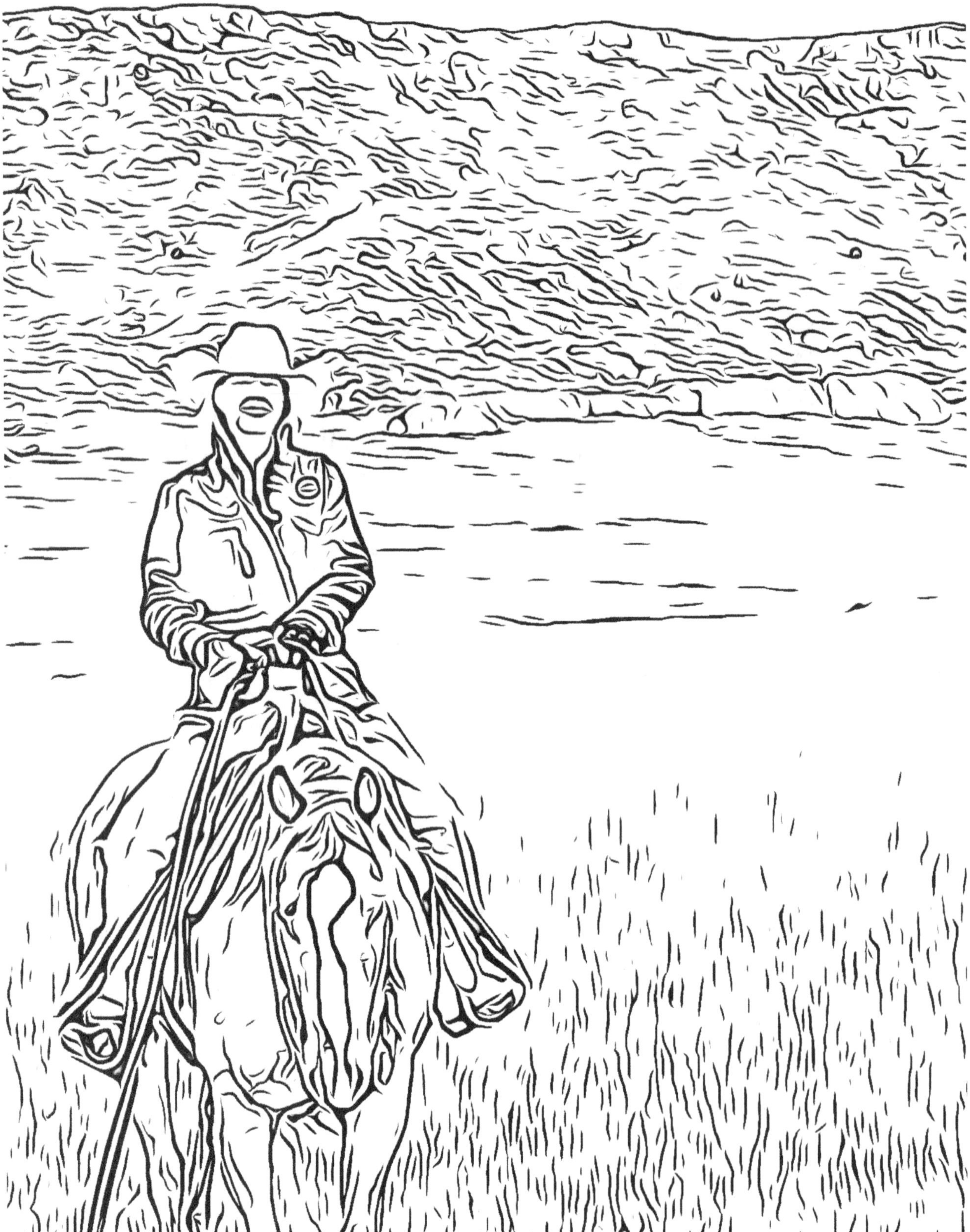

97

98

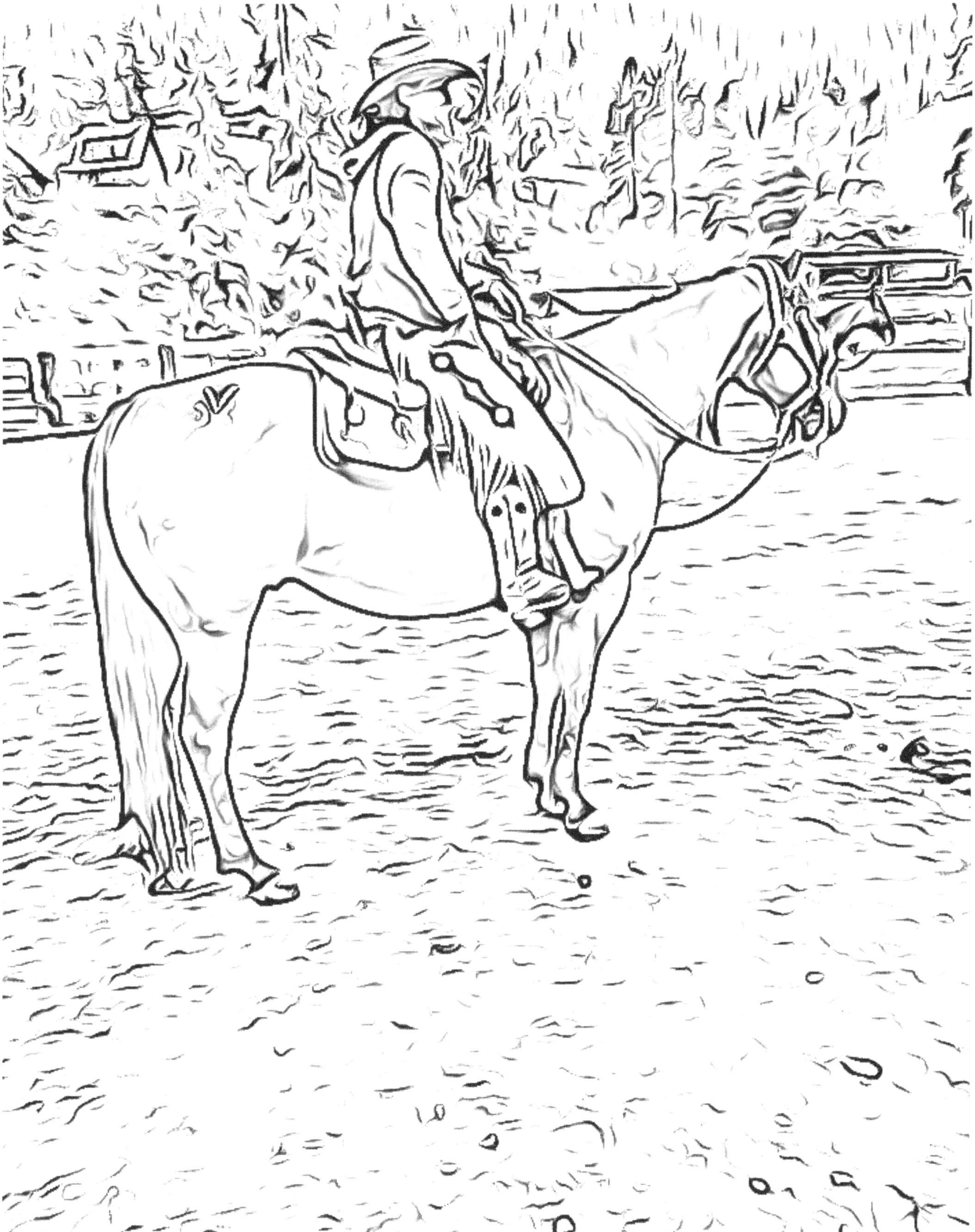

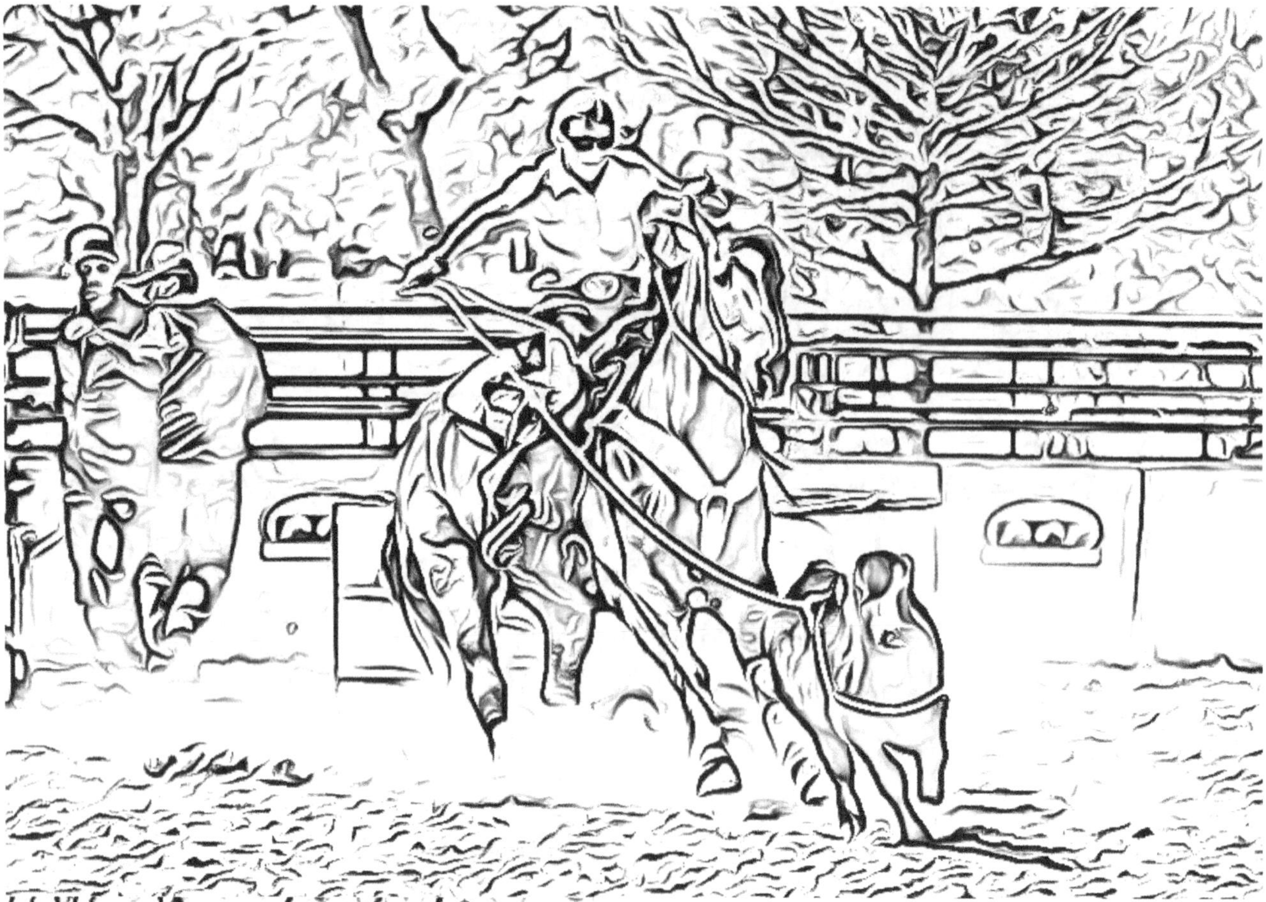

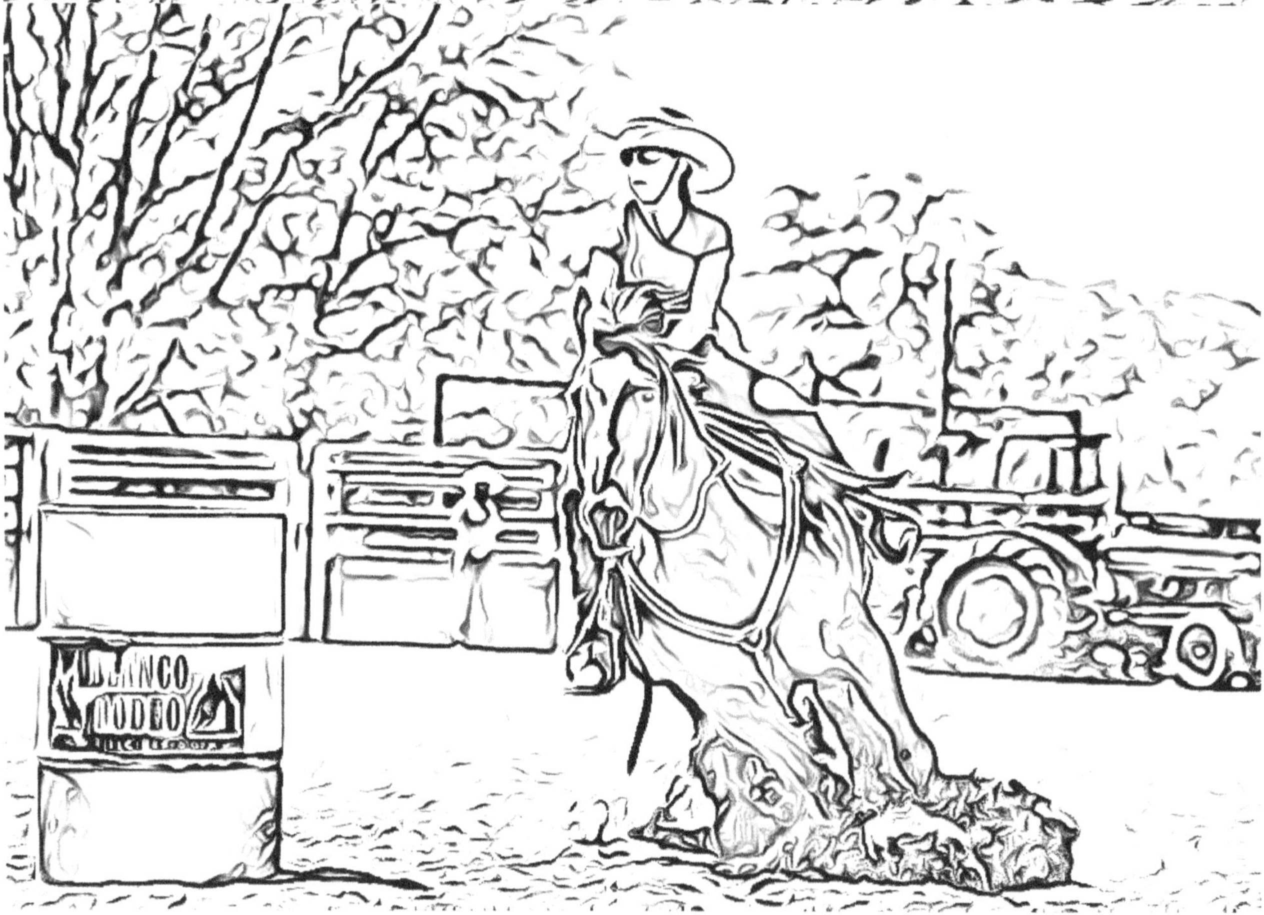

thank you
PHOTOGRAPHER CREDITS

Kenneth Springer Photography
Lexi Smith Media
Boaz Dov Elkes
RM Photos
Traci Davenport Photography
Mike Copeman Photography
Richard Field Levine
Belle Delaney Photography
SKB Ventures LLC - Spotlight on You Video - Photo
Texas Real Sports Photography
PixelWorx Digital Imaging & Graphic Design
AE Photography LLC
Scott Foley Photography
Stacy Berg Photography
Buddy Berry Photography
Roy Ortis Photography
Dale Miller Photography
Lyndsey Lamell Photography
Lincoln Harris Photography
Sam-Sin Photography
Ramona Swift Photography
Spur of the Moment - Nancy Wilkins
Sarai Angelle - Dream Fast Media
Kierce Photography
Ruehle Photographix LLC
Kate B Creative
Tayler Bicandi Media

Made in the USA
Middletown, DE
16 January 2025